Russian, German & Polish
food & cooking

Russian, German & Polish
food & cooking

over 185 traditional recipes from the Baltic to the Black Sea,
shown step-by-step in more than 750 colour photographs

contributing editor: Lesley Chamberlain
recipe authors: Catherine Atkinson and Trish Davies

HERMES
HOUSE

This edition is published by Hermes House

Hermes House is an imprint of Anness Publishing Ltd
Hermes House, 88–89 Blackfriars Road, London SE1 8HA
tel. 020 7401 2077; fax 020 7633 9499; info@anness.com

A CIP catalogue record for this book is available from the British Library.

Publisher: Joanna Lorenz
Editor: Margaret Malone
Designer: Julie Francis
Copy Editor: Jo Lethaby
Photography: Dave Jordan and Ian Garlick
Food for Photography: Sara Lewis, assisted by Julie Beresford and
Clare Lewis, assisted by Sascha Brodie
Styling: Marion McLornan and Shannon Beare
Illustrators: Angela Wood (artworks) and David Cook (maps)
Editorial Reader: Joy Wotton
Production Controller: Julie Hadingham

Previously published as *Russian, Polish and German Cooking*

Front cover main image shows Stuffed Vine Leaves, for recipe see page 226

1 3 5 7 9 10 8 6 4 2

Notes

Standard spoon and cup measures are level.

Large eggs are used unless otherwise stated.

CONTENTS

INTRODUCTION

From the Baltic Sea in the north to the Black Sea in the south, the cooking of Eastern Europe brings to mind hearty, flavorful dishes. Due to not always fruitful soil, everyday fare has been greatly influenced by the need to overcome long hard winters. The results, however, are wonderfully surprising. Though many common characteristics are shared, traditional food from Eastern Europe can be surprisingly diverse and subtle in its ingenious use of ingredients and flavors.

Germans, Czechs, Hungarians, Poles, Ukrainians and Russians are all proud of their robust cuisines, which have changed little during this century. Their repertoires include soups and stews of universal renown and the most nourishing bread to be found in the world. The cooking is long and slow, and the flavors, derived from vegetables and fish, are well developed.

While the southern cuisines of the Balkan countries of Romania, Bulgaria and former Yugoslavia share many flavors with their northern neighbors, the long hot summers and richer soil produce an enviable vegetable harvest. The region's dishes provide colorful contrasts to northern ones and are altogether spicier, with many flavors and textures influenced by Italy, Greece and Turkey.

It is no exaggeration therefore to say that the cooking of Eastern Europe takes in the flavors and traditions of half the world.

HISTORY AND REGIONAL CHARACTERISTICS

The great European empires played a major part in dividing this region, and this book, into three roughly geo-political areas: Russia, Ukraine and Poland; Germany, Austria, Hungary and the Czech Republic; the Balkans and the east Adriatic coast.

Eastern Europe is a major area on the food map. Russian cooking boasts rich sour soups, pancakes and porridges, and yeast-leavened baked goods. Central European cooking is the legacy of the Austro-Hungarian Empire with, as one of its jewels, its rich café culture. The cakes and pastries of Central Europe, such as *Linzertorte* and *Dobos Torta*, are world famous.

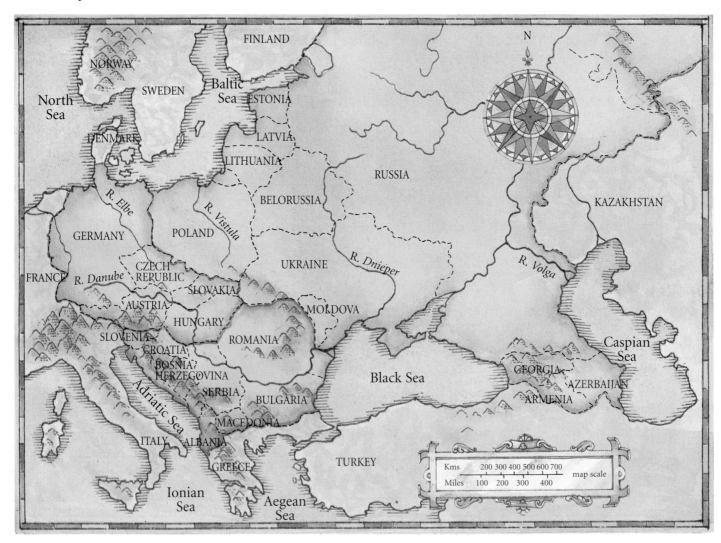

The spicier cooking of the Balkan countries, from Serbia in the west to Bulgaria in the east, and along the east Adriatic, comprises the third region, all of which was formerly part of the Ottoman Empire. These divisions, however, are not meant to be taken as set in stone, and there is much movement between these three regions. The food of countries such as Hungary, Slovakia and Croatia, for example, draws on both Balkan and Central European influences, and German cooking provides the gateway to the rest of Europe.

FROM NORTH TO SOUTH

In northeast Europe, rye is the main grain crop, rather than wheat, hence the customary black bread that has become a favorite around the world for its taste and nutritional value. Typical vegetables from Germany to Russia are root crops: carrots, turnips, onions, potatoes, kohlrabi, beets and horseradish. Cabbages and flat-leaf parsley are also universal, while the most common fruits are apples and berries. The northeastern European diet has for centuries relied on preserved versions of these vegetables and fruits in winter. Hence, alongside pickled vegetables are high-quality jams, which are used for making excellent sweet pies and cakes. The tradition of annual jam-making is still widely practiced in the home.

The northern half of Eastern Europe is also where the great mushrooming cultures have thrived, and a number of much-loved dishes, such as soups and stews, feature these miraculous fruits of the damp autumn forest, from which so much ancient folklore stems.

Other tastes also belong wholly and uniquely to Eastern Europe. They include, above all, the use of fresh dill and sour cream in salads and soups, light rye bread with caraway seeds and home-baked goods, ranging from apple strudels, and poppy seed rolls to cheesecakes. By contrast, the richer soil and the long hot summers of the Balkan countries in the south mean that vegetables and fruit more often associated with the Mediterranean, such as zucchini, eggplant and bell peppers, melons, tomatoes, apricots and peaches, grow in abundance.

Top: This poppy seed roll is a classic example of Polish sweet yeast baking.

Left: Eastern Europe can be examined in a multitude of ways—historically, culturally, geographically, politically— and via its grand culinary traditions.

Right: Fruit picking in Skopje, Macedonia. Don't be surprised to find apple jam on the breakfast table down south.

Some of the more unusual recipes in this book are all-vegetable dishes from the Balkans, for example, rice and zucchini from Romania and vegetable casseroles from Serbia and Bulgaria. Rice is also prominent in Balkan desserts, often baked into a pudding and flavored with the rose water that goes into many other dishes as well.

Other local ingredients, rarely seen further north, include chestnuts, walnuts and sesame seeds, again used mainly in desserts.

OUTSIDE INFLUENCES

In the world of food, geographical and ethnic boundaries are often blurred. The beet soup variously called *borscht* and *barczsz* is a well-known feature of Polish, Ukrainian and Russian tables, and claimed by each country as its own creation. The cooking of countries such as Hungary and Romania combines neighboring German and Middle Eastern elements with the use of a wide range of produce, including bell peppers, eggplant and brine cheeses. In Polish cooking, hints of Italian cuisine can be seen.

Ingredients have been transplanted and imported from other parts of the world, too. The many festive cookies and honey cakes to be found in the Polish, German and Russian repertoires bear witness to the spice trade with the East, which traveled overland from China. It took the active

example of Prussian Emperor Frederick the Great in the early 18th century to encourage his people to eat the potato, newly arrived from the New World. Imported tomatoes, oranges and lemons also brought a welcome lift and color to the local food.

THE ROLE OF RELIGION

Religion has played a part, too, in the region's cooking. In all the countries included in this book the Church has had its influence on cooking. The Orthodox tradition, in particular, imposed fasting or semi-fasting through much of the year, so there is a wide Lenten repertoire in Russian cooking. This is one of the reasons why Russian cuisine became adept at developing satisfying meat-free dishes from a restricted number of ingredients, like cabbage and beets. Dishes intended for days of fasting are thus the product of a highly developed culinary imagination. This is certainly true of *blini*, the Russian buckwheat pancakes, which are served with smoked fish

Top: Bulgarian rice pudding, with rose water from the Valley of the Roses.

Left: Russians drinking tea made using a traditional samovar, c. 1913.

or caviar during Carnival Week or *Maslenitsa*. The semi-fast of the week leading up to Lent, during which meat was avoided, became a celebration of other good things.

Similarly, during their long sojourn in that part of the world, Jewish cooks adapted many East European dishes to cope with the restrictions imposed by keeping a kosher kitchen, especially the injunction against eating pork. The lasting influence of Jewish cooking can be seen, for instance, in recipes for potato pancakes and carp dishes.

TYPICAL FARE

The style of cooking that begins in Germany and moves east is far removed from the gastronomic traditions of western Europe. French-style sauces, for example, are conspicuously absent. Cheese is never offered after the main course, nor is salad served as a separate digestive course. Rather, cheeses and salads of both raw and cooked vegetables tend to appear among the copious appetizers that make up the cold table at the start of a meal.

The ritual of the cold table is one of the great pleasures of Eastern Europe. It is here that many of their most famous dishes appear; caviar is just one example. Salted and pickled herring are also favorites, from Germany through Poland and into Russia, as are sausages. The cold table is especially well endowed with spicy, garlicky, salami-style sausages.

Despite the pressures of the working day, lunch is still the preferred big meal for families from Germany to Russia. In the Czech lands or Poland, people sit down to soup and a main course, perhaps

with a salad alongside, followed by a dessert. Further south, in Bulgaria, for example, families might enjoy tomatoes and cucumber dressed with yogurt, and pork kebabs accompanied by fresh bread, with ice cream to follow.

For the main course on special occasions, there are many fabulous recipes for beef casseroles and roasts, as well for chicken and goose. For everyday purposes, however, pork is the most popular meat. It is cooked in thin slices German schnitzel-style, ground into rissoles or cooked as kebabs.

Fresh cucumber salad or, even better, pickled cucumbers are a popular complement to pork. Eastern Europe is justifiably famous for its successful combination of meaty and sour flavors.

BREAD

Since bread is really at the heart of the region's good food, stopping in at the bakery to buy a loaf must be one of the most satisfying food experiences of Eastern Europe. It may be white bread, made partly or

entirely with wheat, which is especially plentiful in the Ukraine. Many other areas rely more on rye than wheat to provide their staple breads. The taste and texture of these dark breads is perhaps what East Europeans miss most of all when they travel.

Yeast-leavened breads and cakes traditionally required time, loving supervision and a carefully controlled wood-fired oven. Endless hours of care were lavished on Russian *kulich* and Polish *babka* at Easter, and German *stollen* at Christmas. The people of Eastern Europe, whose food was tied to religious feasts and fasts as well as the vicissitudes of the harvest and the time of year, distinguished between plain and luxury food— and one way of doing this was to contrast the daily sour black bread with these grand cakes.

As more refined baking became increasingly popular in the towns, white bread made with refined flour, egg breads like the Jewish *challah* and slightly sweet buns were produced during the 19th century.

Right: Delivery of milk in Albania by traditional means.

GRAINS

Besides the grains for making bread, there are others, such as millet, barley and buckwheat (although this is not a true grain), which are used to make *kasha*. In Romania, whole areas of land are given over to corn, which is used to make cornmeal porridge, *mamaliga*, in much the same way as Italians use polenta. Millet and buckwheat are easily cooked into the nourishing porridges, soups and puddings that play an important part in a meatless or low-protein diet.

FISH

Many traditional dishes made use of fish, which were once plentiful in the waterways of the region. The rivers once teemed with fish such as tench, pike and pike-perch, and from the sea came sturgeon and catfish. Environmental pollution has taken a huge toll in East Europe, while global deep-sea fishing has largely replaced locally caught river fish with deep-sea, frozen fish in

the stores. Although the region's fish dishes have grown plainer and more uniform as a result, the recipes included in this book recall those earlier times.

One fish that has maintained its importance over the years is the humble herring. Once the staple fare from Hamburg to Moscow, it is still prepared according to traditional recipes. Fresh herring is traditionally marinated with apples, pepper and oil or preserved in salt, vinegar, allspice berries and bay leaves.

SAUERKRAUT

East European cooking tends to be more sour than savory. Pickled cabbage dishes known as sauerkraut are one successful sour example. The cabbage acquires a particular succulence and strength of flavor from the fermentation process that has made it popular right across the region, from Germany through Bohemia and Poland to Russia, and down into the Balkans.

The most delicious sauerkraut dishes include the famous *bigos*, a Polish dish, and recipes for stuffed cabbage leaves or *golubtsy*.

ALCOHOL

Alcohol is rarely used as an ingredient in East European cooking compared with the French and Italian traditions. In many regions where climate and soil would have supported wine making, it never really flowered in the past, and this is partly due to religious influences. Muslim-dominated southeast Europe certainly did not cook with wine, and these countries have only relatively recently started to produce and export it. Catholic and Protestant lands were more tolerant, and for centuries flowery white wines have been produced and drunk in western and southern Germany, south Bohemia and Moravia. Today, a wide range of

Top: Polish bigos *was originally cooked in the forest for aristocratic hunting parties because it could be successfully reheated over an open fire.*

Left: Baking bread in a wood oven according to traditional peasant methods.

new global market-quality table wines have built on old traditions in Hungary and Romania and encouraged new ones in Bulgaria, Serbia and Montenegro. Even so, these are not wine-drinking cultures such as the Mediterranean.

In Central and Eastern Europe lager beer or spirits such as vodka, brewed from rye or potatoes, are generally the preferred drinks to accompany a meal. The vodka is high quality, as are the excellent fruit brandies characteristic of the southern countries.

HOME COOKING

Until very recently, food right across Eastern Europe was best bought at local markets, where the sauerkraut was weighed out from wooden barrels and the paprika was spooned into newspaper cornets. Live chickens, honey and slabs of curd and brine cheese would all be for sale, alongside stalls selling fruit, vegetables and herbs. The bakery would also not be far away from the marketplace.

As none of the East European cuisines has been restaurant-led, the lucky traveler in Eastern Europe could be invited into a private home to sample local dishes. Whatever the food offered, the guest is always likely to receive a splendid gastronomic welcome.

For the reader at home, this book provides a comprehensive collection of recipes that reflect pride in the traditional tables of each locality. Grouped according to

region, typical dishes suited to both ordinary and elaborate occasions are provided. They can be enjoyed and sampled by any cook anywhere in the world.

Largely due to the region's 50 years of political isolation from market influences, the East European way of eating has gone more or less untouched by modern views of what constitutes a healthy diet. However, the recipes in this book have been lightened and reduced in calories, to suit present-day Western preferences and nutritional concerns.

East European cooking is often economical because it mainly encapsulates peasant culinary traditions. It requires not fancy ingredients, but rather a willingness to put in some time in the kitchen—something that is worth doing in order to create these recipes and reproduce the tastes and textures of really good food.

Top: The much-loved Black Forest Cherry Cake is truly delicious and comes from southern Germany where Kirsch is distilled.

Left: Open-air cafe in Vienna, watercolor by Wilhelm Gause, 1901.

RUSSIA, POLAND AND THE UKRAINE

The cooking of this area forms one of the classic cuisines of world, encapsulating all the characteristics of traditional cooki have remained virtually unchanged for centuries. Be it a hu beet soup or the glories of caviar, the ingredients, flavors and t all show what good cooking really should be.

INTRODUCTION

The region occupied by Russia, Poland and the Ukraine has a tradition of peasant cooking, defined by the tart flavors of sourdough rye bread, pickles and sauerkraut, and complemented by mushrooms, herring, onion and sausage. These simple foods reflect what the often poor soil yielded in the harsh climate, and what could be preserved by traditional means (in salt or vinegar or by drying) for year-round use. Hardy root and vegetable crops, a variety of grains, the flavors of garlic, mustard and horseradish, and sour dairy products, such as yogurt and buttermilk (the Russian *kefir),* were the region's staples. Cabbage and cucumbers, fresh or pickled, were the primary sources of vitamin C in what, for centuries, was a highly restricted diet.

RELIGIOUS INFLUENCES
In Russia and those parts of the Ukraine where the Russian Orthodox Church determined popular eating habits, at least until the beginning of the 20th century, the Church made a virtue out of economic necessity. It divided foods into two groups. For over half the days of the year only Lenten fare was allowed: vegetables, fish and mushrooms. Milk, eggs and meat were permitted on the remaining days.

The result of this intervention was a good number of simple, versatile recipes. A full meal might consist of a cabbage soup with a grain porridge called *kasha.* Meat, if available, would be cooked in the soup but served separately afterward. On full fast days, mushrooms could be substituted for meat to give the soup flavor and perhaps to fill little pies or *pirozhki* to eat alongside it.

Buckwheat pancakes and sour cream, typical of the meat-free Carnival Week, now rank among the best-liked Russian dishes in the world. Russian Easter food, centered on roast suckling pig basted in sour cream and a cake, *kulich,* served with a sweet cream cheese, is a splendidly rich contrast with the simpler Lenten food that precedes it.

In Poland, there are 12 Lenten dishes—to equal the number of apostles—including a beet soup, herring, carp in black sauce and a mushroom dish. Christmas is an important time for the Roman Catholic Church, and the elaborate Polish meal on Christmas Eve is gastronomically typical.

RECENT CHANGES
Two factors in the 19th century began to modernize the East European peasant diet. One was the industrialization that brought peasants into the towns and saw middle-class cooking influenced by cosmopolitan ideas. The other was the impact of the eating habits of the royal courts on the cuisines of both Russia and Poland, which eventually filtered down through the aristocracy to the bourgeoisie.

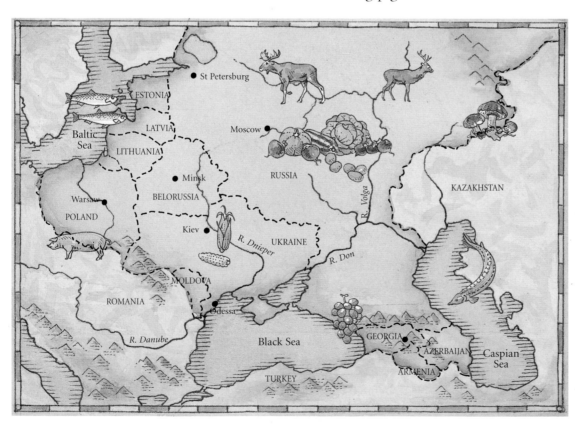

Left: The recipes in this section cover an area that stretches from the Baltic Sea in the north to the Caspian and Black Seas in the south. From Russia, the Baltic countries and Poland in the north, through the Ukraine and down to the edge of Turkey and the Middle East, these recipes reflect the wonderful diversity and the overall defining culinary characteristics of classic East European food.

Right: Open-air cooking on a large scale in Yakut, former USSR.

THE ROYAL COURTS

The Polish court flourished in the 16th century, when Poland's empire stretched from the Baltic to the Black Sea, and the educated minority enjoyed an artistic and political culture, rich in contacts with Renaissance Europe. The Italian connection was particularly strong, due to the Italian-born Queen Bona Sforza who brought with her an entourage and ideas about cooking when she married King Sigismund in 1518. As a consequence, southern European vegetables were planted in the garden of the Royal Court at Krakow. Bona Sforza is also associated with Polish ice cream, pasta and cakes—Polish *babka* is really a first cousin to Italian *panettone*.

In the 19th century, access to French cook books led to Polish cooking becoming richer than Russian in, for example, sauces and composite tastes. At the same time, however, the Russian upper classes also felt under constant pressure to "Frenchify" their own cooking. The court and aristocracy mainly employed French chefs to produce elaborate dishes, replete with butter and cream. Antonïn Carême, as cook to Alexander I (Tsar 1801–25), began a task that was continued by four generations of foreign chefs up to the Russian Revolution.

Generally, however, there was always opposition to this outside influence, and patriotic palates preferred the traditional breads, grains and soups. One such example is *borscht*, the famous beet soup, whose origin cannot be fixed within any present-day national confines. It can be served as a consommé or as a thick soup.

By contrast, the Russian cold table, originally borrowed from Scandinavia during the reign of the

great Westernizing tsar, Peter I (Tsar 1682-1725), has been wholly incorporated into the national cuisine as the classic first course. Consisting of a variety of

hors d'oeuvres, these *zakuski* dishes, which are washed down with ice-cold vodka, deserve their fame, especially as the jewel of the *zakuski* table is often caviar.

INGREDIENTS

VEGETABLES AND MUSHROOMS

Cucumbers, with a firm texture and full flavor, are either used fresh in salads or pickled in bottles for winter. Other popular vegetables are beets, potatoes, carrots, parsnips and fresh cabbage, all of which grow well in a cold climate and can be stored all year round. Cabbage is also fermented in brine, with spices, to make the widely available sauerkraut. As for scallions, both the white bulbs and the green tips contribute to the characteristic flavor of East European composed salads.

The romance of mushroom hunting belongs to the forests of Eastern Europe, where many varieties are found. Mushrooms are dried for use in soups and sauces, or salted or pickled for snacks with bread and vodka. They are also sautéed fresh in butter and herbs, or sauced with sour cream.

Top left, clockwise from left: pickled beets, sauerkraut, pickled cucumbers, dill pickles and caperberries.

Top right, clockwise: red and white cabbage, beets, cucumbers, mushrooms, parsnips, potatoes and carrots.

Right, from top left: Black and red lumpfish roe, salmon caviar, pike, salmon, carp and herring.

FISH

The most celebrated fish of this region belong to the sturgeon family. Of this family, both the beluga and the sevruga produce the highly prized black caviar. Freshwater salmon varieties are also very important, both for their firm flesh and for the "red" caviar so often seen on *zakuski* tables. Carp is traditional in Poland and is nowadays farmed. Herring is popular everywhere, although increasingly only the canned product is available. Pike, perch and pike-perch are the grand old river fish, yielding a firm white flesh that is suitable for pies and baked fish dishes.

DAIRY PRODUCTS

Sour cream takes the place of oil in dressing East European salads of raw and cooked vegetables. It is the essential accompaniment to soups and pancakes and the basis for modern sauced dishes such as Beef Stroganov. It is also used in baking cakes and cookies.

The traditional East European cheeses are made with cow's milk and are young and mild. Curd cheese is used to make savory dips and *paskha*, the sweet Easter treat. Curd cheese can be used alone or with other ingredients to make savory or sweet patties; it is also used to stuff pasta and pies, and forms the basis for the traditional cheesecake. *Brinza*, similar to Greek feta, is a brine cheese common all over Eastern and Central Europe that appears in appetizers and pies.

MEAT DISHES

Suckling pig is a traditional Russian delicacy, as is the game bird called *ryabchik*, or hazel-hen. Plentiful use is made of beef for braising and stewing. Polish sausage is made of top-quality pork and veal, flavored with garlic and mustard seed.

GRAINS

The Russian word *kasha* and the related words in Polish and Ukrainian denote any cooked grain. Semolina, millet, oats and buckwheat are eaten at breakfast, usually cooked in water or milk and served with butter. Buckwheat, rice, millet or barley accompany savory dishes. Buckwheat, actually a relative of the rhubarb family rather than a grain, is cooked into *kasha*, and its flour is used to make traditional Shrovetide pancakes, or *blini*. It grows prolifically in Eastern Europe, and its recognizable smoky taste is characteristic of traditional peasant cooking.

Sourdough breads from this area have a distinctive, satisfying quality, thanks to their being made with rye flour by a sour fermentation process. This produces long-lasting loaves with excellent digestive properties, ranging from straw-colored bread to the distinctly black Russian *borodinsky*, which is made with molasses and has its crust studded with coriander seeds.

HERBS, SPICES AND OTHER FLAVORINGS

Dill, the most common herb in Eastern and Central European cooking, adds a distinct freshness to pickles as well as to salads and cooked dishes. The feathery leaves needed for authentic cooking lose much of their taste when dried, so they should always be used fresh. The pungent seeds can be used in sauerkraut dishes and stews. Parsley, of the pungent, flat-leaf variety, is also widely used in soups and salads and as a garnish, while the root adds flavor to stocks and soup bases. Fresh garlic adds piquancy to soups and stews, while mustard and horseradish give bite to fish and meat dishes.

FRUIT

East Europe has a strong tradition of domestic jam-making and bottling every available fruit and vegetable, from excellent plum jam to pickled spiced tomatoes. Less solid jams, which preserve the whole fruits, such as Russian black

currant *varen'ye*, are traditionally served in a small saucer with tea, or to accompany a breakfast bowl of semolina *kasha*.

DRINKS

Russians drink tea that is either imported from the Far East or grown in Georgia. The tea is brewed in a small pot on top of the samovar, and diluted with water from the urn below. In Poland, under strong Central European and Italian influence, coffee is more popular. As for alcohol, both Poland and Russia claim to be the home of vodka, which has been made in Eastern Europe since at least the 15th century. Distilled, ideally from rye, it is then purified and water is added. Small additions of barley, oats, buckwheat or wheat, herbs and tree bark give more flavor. Additions to the finished vodka make for specialties such as pepper vodka, which is used as a remedy for colds. Plain vodka is best for the *zakuski* table, however, served ice cold and downed in a single gulp.

Top, clockwise from back: dill, flat-leaved parsley, sour cream, cream, horseradish and fresh garlic bulbs.

Left, clockwise from top left: buckwheat flour, semolina, whole rolled porridge oats, pot barley, millet and raw buckwheat (center).

SOUPS AND APPETIZERS

The classic soups of Eastern Europe have remained unchanged for centuries. Shchi, based on cabbage, is a north Russian specialty, while borscht is made from beets and is popular in the south and throughout Poland and the Ukraine. The balance of sweet and sour is typical, with the use of fermented juice or pickled vegetables. Many hors d'oeuvres served in the west originated as Russian appetizers. Caviar is probably the most famous of these, traditionally served with small glasses of ice-cold vodka.

Pea and Barley Soup

This thick and warming soup, *Grochówka*, makes a substantial appetizer, or it may be served as a meal in its own right, eaten with hot crusty bread.

INGREDIENTS

Serves 6
1¼ cups yellow split peas
¼ cup pearl barley
7½ cups vegetable or ham stock
2 ounces bacon, cubed
2 tablespoons butter
1 onion, finely chopped
2 garlic cloves, crushed
8 ounces celeriac, cubed
1 tablespoon chopped fresh marjoram
salt and freshly ground black pepper
bread, to serve

1 Rinse the peas and barley in a sieve under cold running water. Put in a bowl, cover with plenty of water and let soak overnight.

2 The next day, drain and rinse the peas and barley. Put them in a large pan, pour in the stock and bring to a boil. Turn down the heat and simmer gently for 40 minutes.

3 Dry-fry the bacon cubes in a frying pan for 5 minutes or until well browned and crispy. Remove with a slotted spoon, leaving the fat behind, and set aside.

4 Add the butter to the frying pan, then the onion and garlic, and cook gently for 5 minutes. Add the celeriac and cook for another 5 minutes, or until the onion is just starting to color.

5 Add the softened vegetables and bacon to the pan of stock, peas and barley. Season lightly with salt and pepper, then cover and simmer for 20 minutes or until the soup is thick. Stir in the marjoram, add extra black pepper to taste and serve with bread.

Borscht

Beets are the main ingredient in *Borscht*, and their flavor and color dominate this well-known soup. It is a classic of both Russia and Poland.

INGREDIENTS

Serves 4–6

2 pounds uncooked beets, peeled
2 carrots, peeled
2 celery stalks
3 tablespoons butter
2 onions, sliced
2 garlic cloves, crushed
4 tomatoes, peeled, seeded and chopped
1 bay leaf
1 large parsley sprig
2 cloves
4 whole peppercorns
5 cups beef or chicken stock
²⁄₃ cup beet *kvas* (see *Cook's Tip*) or the liquid from pickled beets
salt and freshly ground black pepper
sour cream, garnished with snipped fresh chives or sprigs of dill, to serve

1 Cut the beets, carrots and celery into fairly thick strips. Melt the butter in a large pan and cook the onions over low heat for 5 minutes, stirring occasionally.

3 Add the garlic and chopped tomatoes to the pan and cook, stirring, for 2 more minutes.

5 Add the muslin bag to the pan with the stock. Bring to a boil, reduce the heat, cover and simmer for 1¼ hours or until the vegetables are very tender. Discard the bag. Stir in the beet *kvas* and season. Bring to a boil. Ladle into bowls and serve with sour cream garnished with chives or dill.

2 Add the beets, carrots and celery and cook for another 5 minutes, stirring occasionally.

4 Place the bay leaf, parsley, cloves and peppercorns in a piece of muslin and tie with string.

COOK'S TIP

Beet *kvas*, fermented beet juice, adds an intense color and a slight tartness. If unavailable, peel and grate 1 beet, add ²⁄₃ cup stock and 2 teaspoons lemon juice. Bring to a boil, cover and set aside for 30 minutes. Strain before using.

Fresh Cabbage Shchi

This version of Russia's national dish is made from fresh cabbage rather than sauerkraut.

INGREDIENTS

Serves 4–6
1 small turnip
2 carrots
3 tablespoons butter
1 large onion, sliced
2 celery stalks, sliced
1 white cabbage, about 1½ pounds
5 cups beef stock
1 tart apple, cored, peeled
   and chopped
2 bay leaves
1 teaspoon chopped fresh dill
2 teaspoons pickled cucumber juice
   or lemon juice
salt and freshly ground black pepper
fresh herbs, to garnish
sour cream and black bread, to serve

1 Cut the turnip and carrots into matchstick strips. Melt the butter in a large pan and stir-fry the turnip, carrot, onion and celery for 10 minutes.

2 Shred the cabbage, and add to the pan with the stock, apple, bay leaves and dill and bring to a boil. Cover and simmer for 40 minutes or until the vegetables are really tender.

3 Remove the bay leaves, then stir in the pickled cucumber juice or lemon juice and season with plenty of salt and pepper. Serve hot, garnished with fresh herbs and accompanied by sour cream and black bread.

Sorrel and Spinach Soup

This is an excellent Russian summer soup. If sorrel is unavailable, use double the amount of spinach instead and add a dash of lemon juice to the soup just before serving.

INGREDIENTS

Serves 4
2 tablespoons butter
8 ounces sorrel, washed and
   stalks removed
8 ounces young spinach, washed and
   stalks removed
1 ounce fresh horseradish, grated
3 cups *kvas* or cider
1 pickled cucumber, finely chopped
2 tablespoons chopped fresh dill
8 ounces cooked fish, such as pike,
   perch or salmon, skinned and boned
salt and freshly ground black pepper
sprig of dill, to garnish

1 Melt the butter in a large pan. Add the sorrel and spinach leaves and fresh horseradish. Cover and gently cook for 3–4 minutes or until the leaves are wilted.

2 Spoon into a food processor and process into a fine purée. Ladle into a tureen or bowl and stir in the *kvas* or cider, cucumber and dill.

3 Chop the fish into bite-size pieces. Add to the soup, then season with plenty of salt and pepper. Chill for at least 3 hours before serving, garnished with a sprig of dill.

--- COOK'S TIP ---

Kvas is a Russian beer made by fermenting wheat, rye and buckwheat.

Mixed Mushroom Solyanka

The tart flavors of pickled cucumber, capers and lemon add extra bite to this rich soup.

INGREDIENTS

Serves 4

2 onions, chopped
5 cups vegetable stock
6 cups mushrooms, sliced
4 teaspoons tomato paste
1 pickled cucumber, chopped
1 bay leaf
1 tablespoon capers in brine, drained
pinch of salt
6 peppercorns, crushed
lemon zest curls, green olives and
  sprigs of flat-leaf parsley, to garnish

1 Put the onions in a large pan with ¼ cup of the stock. Cook, stirring occasionally, until the liquid has evaporated.

2 Add the remaining vegetable stock with the sliced mushrooms, bring to a boil, cover and simmer gently for 30 minutes.

3 In a small bowl, blend the tomato paste with 2 tablespoons of stock.

4 Add the tomato paste to the pan with the pickled cucumber, bay leaf, capers, salt and peppercorns. Cook gently for 10 more minutes.

5 Ladle the soup into warmed bowls and sprinkle lemon zest curls, a few olives and a sprig of flat-leaf parley on each bowl before serving.

Grandfather's Soup

This soup derives its name from the fact that it is easily digested and therefore thought to be suitable for the elderly.

INGREDIENTS

Serves 4
1 large onion, finely sliced
2 tablespoons butter
12 ounces potatoes, peeled and diced
3¾ cups beef stock
1 bay leaf
salt and freshly ground black pepper

For the drop noodles
⅔ cup self-rising flour
pinch of salt
1 tablespoon butter
1 tablespoon chopped fresh parsley,
  plus a little extra to garnish
1 egg, beaten
chunks of bread, to serve

1 In a wide heavy pan, cook the onion in the butter gently for 10 minutes or until it begins to brown.

2 Add the diced potatoes and cook for 2–3 minutes, then pour in the stock. Add the bay leaf, salt and pepper. Bring to a boil, then reduce the heat, cover and simmer for 10 minutes.

COOK'S TIP

Use potatoes, with a floury texture, such as King Edward or Maris Piper.

3 Meanwhile, make the noodles. Sift the flour and salt into a bowl and rub in the butter. Stir in the parsley, then add the egg to the flour mixture and mix into a soft dough.

4 Drop half-teaspoonfuls of the dough into the simmering soup. Cover and simmer gently for another 10 minutes. Ladle the soup into warmed soup bowls, sprinkle on a little parsley, and serve immediately with chunks of bread.

Eggs with Caviar

Caviar is the roe from huge sturgeon fish that swim in the Caspian Sea. It is often served on its own, in a bowl set over crushed ice, with a glass of chilled vodka. Alternatively, it may be used sparingly, as in this Ukrainian recipe, as a garnish.

INGREDIENTS

Serves 4
6 eggs, hard-boiled and halved,
    lengthwise
4 scallions, very finely sliced
2 tablespoons mayonnaise
¼ teaspoon Dijon mustard
2 tablespoons caviar or
    black lumpfish roe
salt and freshly ground black pepper
small sprigs of dill, to garnish
watercress, to serve

1 Remove the yolks from the halved eggs. Mash the yolks into a smooth paste in a bowl with the scallions, mayonnaise and mustard. Mix well and season with salt and pepper.

2 Fill the egg whites with the yolk mixture and arrange them on a serving dish. Spoon a little caviar or roe on top of each before serving with watercress.

TYPES OF CAVIAR

Beluga is the largest member of the sturgeon family, and the eggs are a pearly-gray color. **Oscietra** comes from a smaller sturgeon, and the eggs have a golden tinge. **Sevruga** caviar is less expensive than other types, as it produces eggs at a much younger age. **Lumpfish roe,** not a true caviar, has black or orange eggs. **Salmon roe**, from the red salmon, has large, translucent pink-orange eggs.

Eggplant "Caviar"

The word "caviar" is used to describe spreads and dips made from cooked vegetables. The eggplant is the vegetable most widely used in this way, and many Ukrainian families have their own secret recipe.

INGREDIENTS

Serves 4–6
3 pounds eggplant
1 onion, very finely chopped
1 garlic clove, crushed
5 tablespoons olive oil
1 pound tomatoes, peeled and chopped
1 teaspoon lemon juice
⅔ cup plain yogurt
1 teaspoon salt
freshly ground black pepper
scallion slices, to garnish
toasted bread sticks, to serve

1 Preheat the oven to 350°F. Put the eggplant on an oiled rack over a roasting pan. Bake for 25–30 minutes or until soft. Let cool.

2 Meanwhile, sauté the finely chopped onion and garlic in 1 tablespoon of the oil for 10 minutes.

3 Using a spoon, remove the baked eggplant flesh, then purée in a food processor until smooth. With the motor running, add the remaining oil.

4 Spoon into a bowl. Stir in the onions, tomatoes, lemon juice and yogurt, salt and pepper to taste. Cover with plastic wrap and chill for 4 hours. To serve, garnish with scallions and accompany with toasted bread sticks.

Herring Pâté

Vast amounts of herring are fished in the Baltic Sea to the north of Poland. A traditional Polish hors d'oeuvre, *Pasta Śledziowa* is usually served with tiny glasses of ice-cold vodka.

INGREDIENTS

Serves 4
2 fresh herrings, filleted
¼ cup butter, softened
1 teaspoon creamed horseradish sauce
freshly ground black pepper

To serve
4 slices rye bread
1 small onion, cut into rings
1 red apple, cored and sliced
1 tablespoon lemon juice
3 tablespoons sour cream

1 Chop the herrings into pieces and put in a food processor with the butter, horseradish sauce and pepper. Process until smooth.

2 Spoon the herring pâté into a bowl. Cover with plastic wrap and chill for at least 1 hour.

3 Serve the pâté on rye bread, with onion rings and apple slices, tossed in lemon juice. Top with a little sour cream and garnish with dill.

Little Crackers

These savory Polish crackers, *paluszki*, are delicious served warm or cold with soup or dips, or on their own as a snack.

INGREDIENTS

Makes 30
8 tablespoons butter, softened
1⅓ cups mashed potatoes
1¼ cups all-purpose flour, plus extra for dusting
½ teaspoon salt
1 egg, beaten
2 tablespoons caraway seeds

1 Preheat the oven to 425°F. Put the butter and mashed potatoes in a large bowl. Sift the flour and salt into the bowl, then mix into a soft dough.

2 Knead the dough on a lightly floured surface for a few seconds, or until smooth. Wrap in plastic wrap and chill for 30 minutes.

3 Roll out the potato dough on a lightly floured surface until ⅓ inch thick. Brush with beaten egg, then cut into 1 × 3-inch strips. Transfer to an oiled baking sheet and sprinkle with caraway seeds.

4 Bake for 12 minutes or until lightly browned. Transfer to a wire rack and let cool. Store in an airtight container.

Pirozhki

...ozhki are a great favorite of old and young alike. They look splendid piled high and golden brown.

INGREDIENTS

Makes 35
2 cups all-purpose flour
½ teaspoon salt
½ teaspoon sugar
1 teaspoon active dry yeast
2 tablespoons butter, softened
1 egg, beaten, plus a little extra
6 tablespoons warm milk

For the filling
1 small onion, finely chopped
6 ounces ground chicken
1 tablespoon sunflower oil
5 tablespoons chicken stock
2 tablespoons chopped fresh parsley
pinch of grated nutmeg
salt and freshly ground black pepper

1 Sift the flour, salt and sugar into a large bowl. Stir in the yeast, then make a well in the center.

2 Add the butter, egg and milk and mix into a soft dough. Turn onto a lightly floured surface and knead for 10 minutes, until smooth and elastic.

3 Put the dough in a clean bowl, cover with plastic wrap and set in a warm place to rise for 1 hour or until the dough has doubled in size.

4 Meanwhile, stir-fry the onion and chicken in the oil for 10 minutes. Add the stock and simmer for 5 minutes. Stir in the parsley, nutmeg and salt and pepper. Let cool.

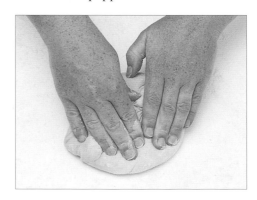

5 Preheat the oven to 425°F. Knead the dough, then roll out until ⅛ inch thick. Stamp out rounds with a 3-inch cutter.

6 Brush the edges with beaten egg. Put a little filling in the middle, then press the edges together. Let rise on oiled baking sheets, covered with oiled plastic wrap, for 15 minutes. Brush with a little more egg. Bake for 5 minutes, then for 10 minutes at 375°F, until well risen.

Buckwheat Blini

Traditionally eaten during the meatless week before Lent, both sweet and savory toppings can be used; sour cream and caviar is the most famous.

INGREDIENTS

Serves 4

²⁄₃ cup all-purpose flour
½ cup buckwheat or
    whole-wheat flour
½ teaspoon salt
1 teaspoon active dry yeast
¾ cup warm milk
2 tablespoons butter, melted
1 egg, separated
3 tablespoons oil

For the toppings

²⁄₃ cup sour cream
2 tablespoons chopped fresh dill
¼ cup red or black lumpfish roe
4 ounces smoked mackerel, skinned,
    boned and flaked
¼ cup unsalted butter, softened
finely grated zest of ½ lemon
shredded lemon zest, to garnish
lemon wedges, to serve

1 Sift the flours and salt into a large bowl, adding any bran left in the sieve. Stir in the yeast, then make a well in the center.

2 Pour in the milk and gradually beat in the flour until smooth. Cover with plastic wrap and let rise for 1 hour or until doubled in size.

3 Stir in the melted butter and egg yolk. Whisk the egg white in a bowl until stiff and then gently fold in. Cover and let stand for 20 minutes.

4 Heat 1 tablespoon of the oil in a large, heavy frying pan over medium heat and drop in about 4 spoonfuls of batter. Cook for 1–2 minutes or until bubbles appear on top.

5 Turn them over and cook for another 1 minute or until both sides are brown. Remove the *blini* from the pan and keep them moist in a folded clean dish towel.

6 Repeat the process with the remaining batter, adding a little oil to the pan when needed, to make about 24 *blini*. Let cool.

7 Arrange the *blini* on a serving plate. Use the sour cream and chopped dill to top half of the *blini*. Spoon 1 teaspoon lumpfish roe on top of the sour cream and dill.

8 In another bowl, combine the smoked mackerel, butter and lemon zest and use to top the remaining *blini*. Garnish with shredded lemon zest. Serve with lemon wedges.

Olivier Salad

In the 1880s, the French chef, Olivier, opened a restaurant in Moscow called the Hermitage. It became one of the most famous dining clubs in the city, where many innovative dishes were served. Olivier later published a book of everyday Russian cooking and gave his name to this elaborate salad.

INGREDIENTS

Serves 6

2 young grouse or partridges
6 juniper berries, crushed
3 tablespoons butter, softened
2 small onions, each stuck with
   3 cloves
2 strips bacon, halved
10 baby potatoes, unpeeled
1 cucumber
2 Little Gem lettuces, separated
   into leaves
2 eggs, hard-boiled and quartered

For the dressing

1 egg yolk
1 teaspoon Dijon mustard
¾ cup light olive oil
¼ cup white wine vinegar
salt and freshly ground black pepper

1 Preheat the oven to 400°F. Put the grouse or partridges in a small roasting pan. Combine the juniper berries and the butter and tuck half the juniper butter and one clove-studded onion into each of the birds.

2 Lay 2 bacon strips over each breast. Roast for 30 minutes or until the juices run only slightly pink when the thigh is pierced with a skewer.

3 Let cool, then cut the meat into 1-inch pieces.

4 Meanwhile, cook the potatoes in boiling salted water for about 20 minutes or until tender. Let cool, then peel and cut into ½-inch slices.

COOK'S TIP

Cold roast beef can be used instead of the game, if you prefer.

5 Cut a few slices of cucumber for garnishing and set aside. Halve the remaining cucumber lengthwise, remove the seeds and dice.

6 To make the dressing, put the egg yolk, mustard and a little salt and pepper in a small bowl and whisk together. Add the olive oil in a thin stream, whisking constantly until thickened, then stir in the vinegar.

7 Put the pieces of meat, potato and cucumber in a bowl. Pour on half the dressing and mix carefully. Arrange the lettuce leaves on a serving platter and pile the salad in the middle.

8 Garnish with the reserved cucumber slices and the quartered hard-boiled eggs. Serve with the remaining dressing.

MEAT AND POULTRY

Although beef, poultry and game are eaten in Russia, Poland and the Ukraine, pork is by far the most popular meat. Large cuts are usually marinated to produce tender and succulent meat, and pork is the main ingredient in kielbasa, the famous Polish sausage exported all over the world. Throughout the region, frequent food shortages in history have called for ingenuity in making a little go a long way, and many recipes reflect this by cleverly combining a number of meats with herbs, spices and pickled vegetables.

Liver and Bacon Varenyky

There is an old Ukrainian superstition that if *varenyky* are counted, the dough will split and the filling spill out.

INGREDIENTS

Serves 4
1³/₄ cups all-purpose flour
¹/₄ teaspoon salt
2 eggs, beaten
1 tablespoon butter, melted
beaten egg, for sealing
1 tablespoon sunflower oil

For the filling
1 tablespoon sunflower oil
¹/₂ small onion, finely chopped
4 ounces bacon,
  roughly chopped
8 ounces chicken or lamb's liver,
  roughly chopped
2 tablespoons snipped fresh chives,
  plus extra for garnish
salt and freshly ground black pepper

1 Sift the flour and salt into a bowl. Make a well in the center. Add the eggs and butter and mix into a dough.

2 Knead the dough on a lightly floured surface for 2–3 minutes, until smooth. Wrap in plastic wrap and let rest for 30 minutes.

3 For the filling, heat the oil in a pan and cook the onion for 5 minutes. Add the bacon and cook for another 4–5 minutes. Stir in the liver and cook for 1 minute, until browned.

4 Put the liver mixture in a food processor or blender and process until it is finely chopped, but not smooth. Add the snipped chives and season with salt and pepper. Process for a few more seconds.

5 Roll out the dough on a lightly floured surface until ¹/₈ inch thick. Stamp out rounds of dough with a 2-inch cutter.

6 Spoon a teaspoon of filling into the middle of each round. Brush the edges of the dough with beaten egg and fold in half to make half-moon shapes. Let dry on a floured dish towel for 30 minutes.

7 Bring a pan of salted water to a boil. Add the oil, then add the *varenyky*, in batches if necessary. Bring back to a boil and cook them at a gentle simmer for 10 minutes, until tender. Drain well and serve hot, garnished with snipped chives. Serve with fresh capers.

Roast Loin of Pork with Apple Stuffing

A spit-roasted suckling pig, basted with butter or cream and served with an apple in its mouth, was a classic dish for the Russian festive table. This roasted loin with crisp skin makes a less expensive alternative.

INGREDIENTS

Serves 6–8
4 pounds boned loin of pork
1¼ cups dry cider
⅔ cup sour cream
1½ teaspoons sea salt

For the stuffing
2 tablespoons butter
1 small onion, chopped
1 cup fresh white bread crumbs
2 apples, cored, peeled and chopped
scant ½ cup raisins
finely grated zest of 1 orange
pinch of ground cloves
salt and freshly ground black pepper

1 Preheat the oven to 425°F. To make the stuffing, melt the butter in a pan and gently sauté the onion for 10 minutes or until soft. Stir into the remaining stuffing ingredients.

2 Put the pork, rind-side down, on a board. Make a horizontal cut between the meat and outer layer of fat, cutting to within 1 inch of the edges to make a pocket.

3 Push the stuffing into the pocket. Roll up lengthwise and tie with string. Score the rind at ¾-inch intervals with a sharp knife.

───── COOK'S TIP ─────

Do not baste during the final 2 hours of roasting, so that the skin becomes crisp.

4 Pour the cider and sour cream into a casserole, in which the pork just fits. Stir to combine, then add the pork, rind-side down. Cook, uncovered, for 30 minutes.

5 Turn the pork over, so that the rind is on top. Baste with the juices, then sprinkle the rind with sea salt. Cook for 1 hour, basting after 30 minutes.

6 Reduce the oven temperature to 350°F. Cook for another 1½ hours. Let the pork stand for 20 minutes before carving.

Russian Hamburgers

Every Russian family has its own version of this hamburger. The mixture can also be shaped into small round meatballs known as *bitki*, which make irresistible snacks.

INGREDIENTS

Serves 4

2 cups fresh white bread crumbs
3 tablespoons milk
1 pound finely ground beef, lamb or veal
1 egg, beaten
2 tablespoons all-purpose flour
2 tablespoons sunflower oil
salt and freshly ground black pepper
tomato sauce, pickled vegetables and crispy fried onions, to serve

1 Put the bread crumbs in a bowl and spoon on the milk. Let soak for 10 minutes. Add the ground meat, egg, salt and pepper and combine all the ingredients thoroughly.

2 Divide the mixture into 4 equal portions and shape into ovals, each about 4 inches long and 2 inches wide. Coat each with the flour.

3 Heat the oil in a frying pan and fry the burgers for about 8 minutes on each side. Serve with tomato sauce, pickled vegetables and fried onions.

Beef Stroganov

At the end of the 19th century, Alexander Stroganov gave his name to this now well-known Russian dish of beef and onions cooked with cream, and it became his signature dish when entertaining at his home in Odessa. Finely cut French fries are the classic accompaniment.

INGREDIENTS

Serves 4

1 pound fillet or rump steak, trimmed
1 tablespoon sunflower oil
2 tablespoons unsalted butter
1 onion, sliced
1 tablespoon all-purpose flour
1 teaspoon tomato paste
1 teaspoon Dijon mustard
1 teaspoon lemon juice
$^2/_3$ cup sour cream
salt and freshly ground black pepper
fresh herbs, to garnish

1 Place the steak between 2 oiled sheets of plastic wrap. Gently beat with a rolling pin to flatten and tenderize the meat. Cut it into thin strips about 2 inches long.

2 Heat the remaining oil and half the butter in a frying pan and stir-fry the beef over high heat for 2 minutes or until browned. Remove the strips of beef from the pan with a slotted spoon, leaving any juices behind.

3 Melt the remaining butter in the pan and gently sauté the onion for 10 minutes, until soft.

4 Sprinkle on the flour, then stir it in, followed by the tomato paste, mustard, lemon juice and sour cream. Return the beef to the pan and stir until the sauce is bubbling. Season to taste with salt and pepper, and then serve immediately, garnished with fresh herbs, with French fries.

Bigos

Poland's national dish, *bigos*, is best made a day in advance.

INGREDIENTS

Serves 8

¼ cup dried mushrooms
1 cup pitted prunes
8 ounces lean boneless pork
8 ounces lean boneless venison
8 ounces chuck steak
8 ounces *kielbasa* (see Cook's Tip)
¼ cup all-purpose flour
2 onions, sliced
3 tablespoons olive oil
¼ cup dry Madeira
2-pound can or package sauerkraut, rinsed
4 tomatoes, peeled and chopped
4 cloves
2-inch piece cinnamon stick
1 bay leaf
½ teaspoon dill seeds
2½ cups stock
salt and freshly ground black pepper

1 Pour in boiling water to completely cover the dried mushrooms and prunes in a bowl. Set aside for 30 minutes, then drain well.

2 Cut the pork, venison, chuck steak and *kielbasa* sausage into 1-inch cubes, then toss together in the flour. Gently sauté the onions in the oil for 10 minutes. Remove.

3 Brown the meat in the pan in several batches, for about 5 minutes or until well browned; remove and set aside. Add the Madeira and simmer for 2–3 minutes, stirring.

4 Return the meat to the pan with the onion, sauerkraut, tomatoes, cloves, cinnamon, bay leaf, dill seeds, mushrooms and prunes. Pour in the stock and season with salt and pepper.

5 Bring to a boil, cover and simmer gently for 1¾–2 hours or until the meat is very tender. Uncover for the last 20 minutes to let the liquid evaporate, as the stew should be thick. Sprinkle with chopped parsley. Serve immediately with boiled new potatoes, tossed in chopped parsley.

— COOK'S TIP —

Kielbasa is a garlic-flavored pork and beef sausage, but any similar type of continental sausage can be used. Use porcini mushrooms, if possible.

Kovbasa

These Ukrainian pork and beef sausages can be made several days ahead and kept refrigerated.

INGREDIENTS

Serves 6
1 pound pork, such as shoulder
8 ounces chuck steak
4 ounces salt pork
2 eggs, beaten
2 tablespoons *peperivka* (see *Cook's Tip*)
 or pepper vodka
½ teaspoon ground allspice
1 teaspoon salt
about 7½ cups chicken stock
fresh parsley, to garnish
mashed potatoes, to serve

1 Grind the meats and salt pork together, using the coarse blade of a grinder, then grind half the mixture again, this time using a fine blade.

2 Combine both the meat mixtures with the eggs, *peperivka*, allspice and salt. Check the seasoning by frying a small piece of the mixture, then tasting it. Adjust if necessary.

3 Form the meat mixture into 2 sausages, about 8 inches long. Wrap in double buttered muslin and tie securely with string.

4 Bring the stock to a gentle simmer in a large pan. Add the sausages and simmer gently, turning frequently, for 35–40 minutes or until the juices run clear when the sausages are pierced with a fine skewer.

5 Leave the sausages in the stock for 20 minutes, then remove and let cool. Remove the muslin and sauté the sausages in oil to brown them. Garnish with parsley and serve with mashed potatoes, topped with butter.

COOK'S TIP

Spicing whiskey with peppers to make *peperivka* is an old tradition in the Ukraine. Add 3 whole cayenne peppers, pricked all over with a fine skewer, to ⅔ cup whiskey or bourbon and set aside for at least 48 hours.

Field-roasted Lamb

This unusual recipe, originally for mutton slowly roasted over charcoal, comes from the Russian steppes.

INGREDIENTS

Serves 6

4-pound leg of lamb
4 large garlic cloves, cut into slivers
1 teaspoon whole peppercorns
1¼ cups plain yogurt
1 tablespoon olive oil
1 tablespoon chopped fresh dill
1¼ cups lamb or vegetable stock
2 tablespoons lemon juice
potatoes, spinach and carrots,
   to serve

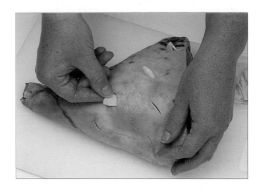

1 Make slits all over the lamb and insert generous slivers of fresh garlic into the slits.

2 Lightly crush the whole peppercorns in a mortar and pestle or with a rolling pin, if preferred.

3 Put the yogurt, oil and crushed peppercorns in a bowl, then add the dill and combine well.

4 Spread the yogurt paste evenly on the lamb. Put the lamb in a glass dish, cover loosely with aluminum foil and then refrigerate the lamb for 1–2 days, turning it twice.

5 Transfer the lamb to a roasting pan and let it come back to room temperature. Preheat the oven to 425°F. Remove the foil. Pour in the stock and lemon juice and cook, uncovered, for 20 minutes.

6 Reduce the oven temperature to 350°F and continue roasting for another 1¼–1½ hours, basting occasionally. Remove from the oven and keep covered in a warm place for 15–20 minutes before carving. Use the juices from the pan to make gravy and serve with roast potatoes, boiled spinach and baby carrots.

Lamb Plov

Plov is the Russian name for this rice dish popular throughout Eastern Europe, known by different names—*pilau* in Turkey and *pilaf* in the Middle East.

INGREDIENTS

Serves 4

scant ¹/₂ cup raisins
¹/₂ cup pitted prunes
1 tablespoon lemon juice
2 tablespoons butter
1 large onion, chopped
1 pound lamb fillet, trimmed and cut
    into ¹/₂-inch cubes
8 ounces lean ground lamb
2 garlic cloves, crushed
2¹/₂ cups lamb or vegetable stock
scant 2 cups long-grain rice
large pinch of saffron threads
salt and freshly ground black pepper
sprigs of flat-leaf parsley, to garnish

1 Put the raisins and prunes in a small bowl and pour in enough water to cover. Add the lemon juice and let soak for at least 1 hour. Drain, then roughly chop the prunes.

2 Meanwhile, heat the butter in a large pan and cook the onion for 5 minutes. Add the lamb fillet, ground lamb and garlic. Cook for 5 minutes, stirring constantly, until browned.

3 Pour in ²/₃ cup of the stock. Bring to a boil, then lower the heat, cover and simmer for 1 hour or until the lamb is tender.

4 Add the remaining stock and bring to a boil. Add the rice and saffron. Stir, then cover and simmer for 15 minutes or until the rice is tender.

5 Stir in the raisins, chopped prunes, salt and pepper. Heat through for a few minutes, then transfer to a warmed serving dish and garnish with sprigs of flat-leaf parsley.

Chicken Bitki

Chicken is one of the most popular meats eaten in Poland. Use guinea fowl to mimic the gamey flavor of Polish chicken.

INGREDIENTS

Makes 12
1 tablespoon butter, melted
4 ounces flat mushrooms,
    finely chopped
1 cup fresh white bread crumbs
12 ounces chicken breasts or guinea
    fowl, ground or finely chopped
2 eggs, separated
1/4 teaspoon grated nutmeg
2 tablespoons all-purpose flour
3 tablespoons oil
salt and freshly ground black pepper
green salad and grated pickled beets,
    to serve

1 Melt the butter in a pan and cook the mushrooms for 5 minutes, until soft and all the juices have evaporated. Let cool.

2 Mix the crumbs, chicken, yolks, nutmeg, salt and pepper and flat mushrooms well.

3 Whisk the egg whites until stiff. Stir half into the chicken mixture, then fold in the remainder.

4 Shape the mixture into 12 even meatballs, about 3 inches long and 1 inch wide. Roll in the flour to coat.

5 Heat the oil in a frying pan and fry the *bitki* for 10 minutes, turning until evenly golden brown and cooked through. Serve hot with a green salad and pickled beets.

Chicken Kiev

This popular recipe is a modern Russian invention. These deep-fried chicken breasts filled with garlic butter should be prepared well in advance to allow time for chilling.

INGREDIENTS

Serves 4
8 tablespoons butter, softened
2 garlic cloves, crushed
finely grated zest of 1 lemon
2 tablespoons chopped fresh tarragon
pinch of freshly grated nutmeg
4 chicken breasts with wing bones
    attached, skinned
1 egg, lightly beaten
2 cups fresh bread crumbs
oil, for deep-frying
salt and freshly ground black pepper
lemon wedges, to garnish
potato wedges, to serve

1 Combine the butter, garlic, lemon zest, tarragon and nutmeg in a bowl. Season to taste with salt and pepper. Shape the butter into a rectangular block about 2 inches long, wrap in aluminum oil and chill for 1 hour.

2 Place the chicken, skinned sides down, on a piece of oiled plastic wrap. Cover with a second piece of plastic wrap and gently beat the pieces with a rolling pin until fairly thin.

3 Cut the butter lengthwise into four pieces and put one in the center of each chicken fillet. Fold the edges over the butter and secure with wooden toothpicks.

4 Put the beaten egg and the bread crumbs into separate small dishes. Dip the chicken pieces first in the beaten egg and then in the bread crumbs to coat evenly. Dip them a second time in egg and crumbs, then put on a plate and refrigerate for at least 1 hour.

5 Heat the oil in a large pan or deep fryer to 350°F. Deep-fry the chicken for 6–8 minutes or until the chicken is cooked and the coating golden brown and crisp. Drain on paper towels and remove the toothpicks. Serve hot, garnished with wedges of lemon and potato wedges.

Chicken and Pork Terrine

Serve this delicate Ukrainian pâté with warm, crusty bread.

INGREDIENTS

Serves 6–8

8 ounces bacon
13 ounces boneless chicken
   breast, skinned
1 tablespoon lemon juice
8 ounces lean ground pork
½ small onion, finely chopped
2 eggs, beaten
2 tablespoons chopped fresh parsley
1 teaspoon salt
1 teaspoon green peppercorns, crushed
fresh green salad, radishes and lemon
   wedges, to serve

1 Preheat the oven to 325°F. Put the bacon on a board and stretch it using the back of a knife so that it can be arranged in over-lapping slices over the bottom and sides of a 2-pound loaf pan.

2 Cut 4 ounces of the chicken into strips about 4 inches long. Sprinkle with lemon juice. Put the rest of the chicken in a food processor or blender with the ground pork and the onion. Process until fairly smooth.

3 Add the eggs, parsley, salt and peppercorns to the meat mixture and process again briefly. Spoon half the mixture into the loaf pan and then level the surface.

4 Arrange the chicken strips on top, then spoon in the remaining meat mixture and smooth the top. Give the pan a couple of sharp taps to knock out any pockets of air.

5 Cover with a piece of oiled aluminum foil and put in a roasting pan. Pour in enough hot water to come halfway up the sides of the loaf pan. Bake for 45–50 minutes, until firm.

6 Let the terrine cool in the pan before turning out and chilling. Serve sliced, with a fresh green salad, radishes and wedges of lemon to squeeze on top.

Roast Duckling with Honey

A sweet-and-sour orange sauce is the perfect foil for this rich-tasting Polish duck recipe, and frying the orange zest intensifies the flavor.

INGREDIENTS

Serves 4
5-pound oven-ready duckling
½ teaspoon ground allspice
1 orange
1 tablespoon sunflower oil
2 tablespoons all-purpose flour
⅔ cup chicken or duck stock
2 teaspoons red wine vinegar
1 tablespoon honey
salt and freshly ground black pepper
watercress and thinly pared orange
    zest, to serve

1 Preheat the oven to 425°F. Using a fork, pierce the duckling all over, except for on the breast, so that the fat runs out during cooking.

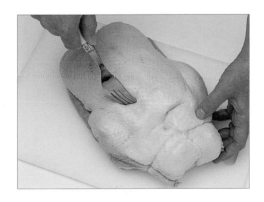

2 Rub all over the skin of the duckling with allspice and sprinkle with salt and pepper.

3 Put the duckling on a rack over a roasting pan and cook for about 20 minutes. Next reduce the oven temperature to 375°F and cook for another 2 hours.

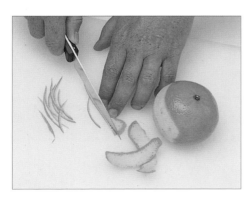

4 Meanwhile, thinly pare the zest from the orange and cut into very fine strips. Heat the oil in a pan and gently fry the orange zest for 2–3 minutes. Squeeze the juice from the orange and set aside.

5 Transfer the duckling to a warmed serving dish and keep warm. Drain off all but 2 tablespoons fat from the pan, sprinkle in the flour and stir well.

6 Stir in the stock, vinegar, honey, orange juice and zest. Bring to a boil, stirring constantly. Simmer for 2–3 minutes. Season the sauce and serve the duckling with watercress and thinly pared orange zest.

FISH

The seas to the north and south and the vast lakes and the rivers that flow across this region provide an abundance of fish, which are cooked in wonderful ways. Russia's most famous export, caviar, comes from the huge sturgeon that swim in the Caspian Sea. The Baltic provides this region with herring, which is served in many guises throughout the year, since it is well suited to pickling. However, freshwater fish predominate. These include eel, perch and salmon, but the favorites are pike and carp—always served on feast days.

Pike and Salmon Mousse

When sliced, this light-textured Russian mousse, *Pate iz Shchuki*, reveals a pretty layer of pink salmon. For a special occasion, serve topped with red salmon caviar.

INGREDIENTS

Serves 8

8 ounces salmon fillets, skinned
2½ cups fish stock
finely grated zest and juice of
  ½ lemon
2 pounds pike fillets, skinned
4 egg whites
2 cups heavy cream
2 tablespoons chopped fresh dill
salt and freshly ground black pepper
red salmon caviar or dill sprig,
  to garnish (optional)

1 Preheat the oven to 350°F. Line a 2-pound loaf pan with waxed paper and brush with oil.

2 Cut the salmon into 2-inch strips. Place the stock and lemon juice in a pan and bring to a boil, then turn off the heat. Add the salmon strips, cover and set aside for 2 minutes. Remove with a slotted spoon.

3 Cut the pike into cubes and process in a food processor or blender until smooth. Lightly whisk the egg whites with a fork. With the motor running, slowly pour in the egg whites, then the cream. Finally, add the lemon zest, dill and seasoning.

4 Spoon half of the pike mixture into the prepared loaf pan.

5 Arrange the poached salmon strips on top, then carefully spoon in the remaining pike mixture.

6 Cover the loaf pan with aluminum foil and put in a roasting pan. Add enough boiling water to come halfway up the sides of the loaf pan. Bake for 45–50 minutes or until firm.

7 Set on a wire rack to cool, then chill for at least 3 hours. Turn out onto a serving plate and remove the lining paper. Serve the mousse cut in slices and garnished with red salmon caviar or a sprig of dill, if desired.

Salmon Kulebyaka

A Russian festive dish in which a layer of moist salmon and eggs sits on a bed of buttery dill-flavored rice, all encased in crisp puff pastry.

INGREDIENTS

Serves 4

¹/₄ cup butter
1 small onion, finely chopped
1 cup cooked long-grain rice
1 tablespoon chopped fresh dill
1 tablespoon lemon juice
1 pound puff pastry, defrosted if frozen
1 pound salmon fillet, skinned and cut into 2-inch pieces
3 eggs, hard-boiled and chopped
beaten egg, for sealing and glazing
salt and freshly ground black pepper
watercress, to garnish

1 Preheat the oven to 400°F. Melt the butter in a pan, add the finely chopped onion and cook gently for 10 minutes or until soft.

2 Stir in the cooked rice, dill, lemon juice, salt and pepper.

3 Roll out the puff pastry on a lightly floured surface into a 12-inch square. Spoon the rice mixture over half the pastry, leaving a ¹/₂-inch border around the edges.

4 Arrange the salmon on top, then sprinkle the eggs in between.

5 Brush the pastry edges with egg and fold it over the filling to make a rectangle, pressing the edges together firmly to seal.

6 Carefully lift the pastry onto a lightly oiled baking sheet. Glaze with beaten egg, then pierce the pastry a few times with a skewer to make holes for the steam to escape.

7 Bake on the middle shelf of the oven for 40 minutes, covering with aluminum foil after 30 minutes. Let cool on the baking sheet before cutting into slices. Garnish with watercress.

Braised Tench and Vegetables

Freshwater tench is the smallest member of the carp family, with a sweet firm flesh and few bones. In this simple Polish recipe, the combination of vegetables can easily be adapted to suit an individual's taste or seasonal availability.

INGREDIENTS

Serves 4

2 pounds tench, filleted
    and skinned
1 tablespoon lemon juice
6 tablespoons butter
1 onion, halved and cut into wedges
1 celery stalk, sliced
1 carrot, halved lengthwise and sliced
1½ cups small button mushrooms,
    halved
¼ cup vegetable stock
salt and freshly ground black pepper

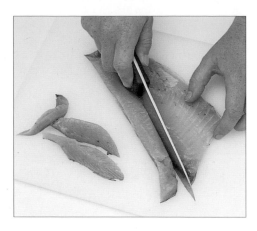

1 Cut the fish fillets into strips about 1 inch wide. Sprinkle them with the lemon juice and a little salt and pepper and set aside.

2 Melt the butter in a large flameproof casserole and cook the onion wedges for 5 minutes. Add the celery, carrot and mushrooms and cook for another 2–3 minutes, stirring to coat in the butter.

3 Pour the stock into the pan. Place the fish on top of the vegetables in a single layer. Cover the casserole with a lid and cook over very low heat for 25–30 minutes, until the fish and vegetables are tender.

—— VARIATION ——

Use small carp in this recipe if desired. Carp has a slightly different flavor.

Flounder in Polish Sauce

This sauce is Polish only in name, not in origin. A mixture of recipes, it is a quick and simple sauce to prepare that goes well with any poached, broiled or steamed fish.

INGREDIENTS

Serves 4

4 flounder fillets, about 8 ounces each
6 tablespoons butter
2 eggs, hard-boiled and
    finely chopped
2 tablespoons chopped fresh dill
1 tablespoon lemon juice
salt and freshly ground black pepper
lemon slices, to garnish
boiled baby carrots, to serve

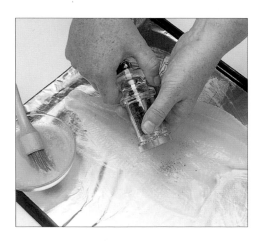

1 Put the fish, skin-side down, on a sheet of greased aluminum foil on a broiler rack. Melt the butter in a small pan and brush a little on the fish. Season with salt and pepper.

2 Broil the fish under medium heat for 8–10 minutes or until just cooked. Transfer to a warmed plate.

3 Add the eggs, dill and lemon juice to the melted butter in the pan. Heat gently for 1 minute. Pour over the fish just before serving. Garnish with lemon slices and serve with boiled baby carrots.

Fish Babka

This fish dish is lightened with egg whites, giving it a soufflé-like texture. It is much more stable, however, and can be turned out of the pan to serve.

INGREDIENTS

Serves 4

12 ounces white fish fillets, skinned and cut into 1-inch cubes
2 ounces white bread, cut into ½-inch cubes
1 cup milk
2 tablespoons butter
1 small onion, finely chopped
3 eggs, separated
¼ teaspoon grated nutmeg
salt and freshly ground black pepper
2 tablespoons chopped fresh dill, plus extra to garnish
sliced zucchini and carrots, to serve

1 Preheat the oven to 350°F. Line a 6¼-cup ovenproof dish with waxed paper and then lightly grease the paper.

2 Place the fish cubes in a bowl. Add the bread, then pour on the milk and let soak while you cook the chopped onion.

3 Melt the butter in a small pan and sauté the onion for 10 minutes, until soft. Cool for a few minutes, then add to the fish and bread with the egg yolks, nutmeg, dill, salt and pepper. Mix well.

4 Whisk the egg whites in a large bowl until stiff, then gently fold into the fish mixture.

5 Spoon the mixture into the dish. Cover with buttered aluminum foil and bake for 45 minutes or until set.

6 Let stand for 5 minutes, then spoon out. Alternatively, loosen with a knife; turn out, remove the paper and cut into wedges. Garnish with dill and serve with zucchini and carrots.

Muscovite Solyanka

This layered fish and vegetable casserole has the same name as one of Russia's classic soups. The name reflects the prevalent "sourness" of the ingredients.

INGREDIENTS

Serves 4

1½ pounds eel, skinned and boned
3¾ cups fish or vegetable stock
5 cups water
4 cups shredded white cabbage
4 tablespoons butter
1 large onion, chopped
2 pickled cucumbers, sliced
12 green olives
1 tablespoon capers, drained
1½ cups fresh white bread crumbs
salt and freshly ground black pepper

1 Cut the eel into large pieces. Bring the stock to a gentle simmer in a large pan, add the eel and cook for 4 minutes. Remove with a slotted spoon. Reserve ⅔ cup of the stock and set aside, leaving the remaining stock in the pan.

2 Pour the water into the pan of stock. Bring to a boil, then add the cabbage. Simmer for 2 minutes, then strain well.

3 Melt half of the butter in the pan. Sauté the onion for 5 minutes.

4 Stir in the strained cabbage and reserved stock, then bring to a boil. Cover with a tight-fitting lid and cook over low heat for 1 hour, until tender. Season with salt and pepper.

5 Preheat the oven to 400°F. Spoon half the cabbage into a baking dish. Top with the eel and the cucumbers. Spoon on the remaining cabbage and any remaining stock.

6 Sprinkle the olives, capers and the bread crumbs on top. Melt the remaining butter and drizzle on the top. Bake for 25–30 minutes or until lightly browned. Garnish with parsley sprigs and serve with boiled potatoes.

Rolled Fish Fillets

Whiting or sea perch can also be used in this dish. Their delicate flavor is complemented by the lemon and thyme.

INGREDIENTS

Serves 4
8 sole fillets, about 7 ounces, skinned
3 tablespoons olive oil
1 tablespoon lemon juice
2 tablespoons butter
2 cups button mushrooms, very finely chopped
4 anchovy fillets, finely chopped
1 teaspoon chopped fresh thyme, plus extra to garnish
2 eggs, beaten
2 cups white bread crumbs
oil, for deep-frying
salt and freshly ground black pepper
broiled endive, to serve

1 Lay the fish fillets in a single layer in a glass dish. Combine the oil and lemon juice and sprinkle on top. Cover with plastic wrap and marinate in the refrigerator for at least 1 hour.

2 Melt the butter in a pan and gently cook the mushrooms for 5 minutes, until tender and all the juices have evaporated. Stir in the chopped anchovies, thyme, salt and pepper.

3 Divide the mixture equally and spread evenly on the fish. Roll up and secure with toothpicks.

COOK'S TIP

To skin the fillets, slice the flesh off of the skin using a sharp knife. Keep the knife parallel to the fish and the skin taut.

4 Dip each fish roll in beaten egg, then in bread crumbs to coat. Repeat this process. Heat the oil to 350°F.

5 Deep-fry in 2 batches for 4–5 minutes or until well browned and cooked through. Drain on paper towels. Remove the toothpicks and sprinkle with thyme. Serve with broiled endive.

Carp with Green Horseradish Sauce

Carp is a freshwater fish used in many Polish dishes, and it is traditional Christmas fare.

INGREDIENTS

Serves 4
1½-pound carp, skinned and filleted
3 tablespoons all-purpose flour
1 egg, beaten
2 cups fresh white bread crumbs
sunflower oil, for frying
salt and freshly ground black pepper
lemon wedges, to serve

For the sauce
½ ounce fresh horseradish, finely grated
pinch of salt
⅔ cup heavy cream
1 bunch of watercress, trimmed and finely chopped
2 tablespoons snipped fresh chives
2 eggs, hard-boiled and finely chopped (optional)

1 Cut the fish into thin strips, about 2½ inches long by ½ inch thick. Season the flour with salt and pepper. Dip the strips of fish in the flour, then in the beaten egg and, finally, in the bread crumbs.

2 Heat ½ inch of oil in a frying pan. Fry the fish in batches for 3–4 minutes, until golden brown. Drain on paper towels and keep warm until all the strips are cooked.

3 For the sauce, put the horseradish, salt, cream and watercress in a small pan. Bring to a boil and simmer for 2 minutes. Stir in the chives and eggs, if using. Serve the sauce with the fish.

Baked Cod with Horseradish Sauce

Baking fish in a sauce keeps it moist. In this Ukrainian recipe, a second, tangy sauce is served alongside for added flavor.

INGREDIENTS

Serves 4
4 thick cod fillets or steaks
1 tablespoon lemon juice
2 tablespoons butter
$^1\!/_4$ cup all-purpose flour, sifted
$^2\!/_3$ cup milk
$^2\!/_3$ cup fish stock
salt and freshly ground black pepper
parsley sprigs, to garnish
potato wedges and chopped scallions, fried, to serve

For the horseradish sauce
2 tablespoons tomato paste
2 tablespoons grated fresh horseradish
$^2\!/_3$ cup sour cream

1 Preheat the oven to 350°F. Place the fish in a buttered ovenproof dish in a single layer. Sprinkle with lemon juice.

2 Melt the butter in a small heavy pan. Stir in the flour and cook for 3–4 minutes, until lightly golden. Stir to stop the flour from sticking to the pan. Remove from heat.

3 Gradually whisk the milk, and then the stock, into the flour mixture. Season with salt and pepper. Bring to a boil, stirring, and simmer for 3 minutes, still stirring.

4 Pour the sauce over the fish and bake for 20–25 minutes, depending on the thickness. Check by inserting a skewer in the thickest part: the flesh should be opaque.

5 For the horseradish sauce, blend the tomato paste and horseradish with the sour cream in a small pan. Slowly bring to a boil, stirring, and then simmer for 1 minute.

6 Pour the horseradish sauce into a serving bowl and serve alongside the fish. Serve the fish hot. Garnish with the parsley sprigs and serve with the potato wedges and fried chopped scallions.

Glazed Pike-perch

This Russian fish dish, with its glistening aspic coating, makes an impressive centerpiece for a formal occasion.

INGREDIENTS

Serves 8–10
5–6-pound whole pike-perch
2 tablespoons sunflower oil
2 bay leaves
8 whole peppercorns
1 lemon, sliced
1¼ cups white wine
1 ounce packet aspic jelly
2 cucumbers, halved and thinly sliced
salt and freshly ground black pepper
dill sprigs and lemon wedges,
   to garnish
mayonnaise, to serve

1 Wash the pike-perch under cold running water. Snip off the fins with sharp scissors. Season the inside of the fish with salt and pepper. Brush the skin with the oil to protect it from heat during cooking.

2 Put the fish on the trivet of a fish kettle or on a rack in a large roasting pan. Add the bay leaves, pepper-corns and lemon slices. Pour in the wine and enough water to cover.

3 Cover with a lid or a piece of oiled aluminum foil. Bring to a boil and simmer very gently for 10 minutes. Turn off the heat and let the pike-perch cool with the lid still on. When cool, peel the skin off the fish, leaving the head and tail intact.

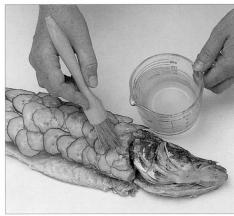

4 Prepare the aspic with boiling water, according to the packet instructions. Cool and brush generously on the fish.

5 Arrange the cucumber slices on the fish, then brush again with aspic. Let set before serving, garnished with dill sprigs and lemon wedges.

COOK'S TIP

A whole fresh salmon or salmon trout can be cooked in exactly the same way.

VEGETABLES, GRAINS AND PASTA

Served on their own or as a side dish, vegetables in Russia, Poland and the Ukraine reflect the cold climate. Cabbage, beets, rutabagas and turnips are the staples, often preserved by salting or pickling. Mushrooms are popular, too, since huge forests cover much of the region, and gathering them is a favorite pastime. Potatoes are also featured, particularly in Polish cooking, although grains, especially buckwheat, rye and barley, are more widely eaten. Surprisingly, stuffed pasta is traditional, usually with meat or cheese fillings.

Potato Cakes

Although not as widely used as grains, potatoes feature often in Polish recipes. They were introduced during the reign of Jan Sobieski, in the 17th century.

INGREDIENTS

Serves 4

1 pound potatoes, peeled and cut into
    large chunks
2 tablespoons butter
1 small onion, chopped
3 tablespoons sour cream
2 egg yolks
$^{1}/_{4}$ cup all-purpose flour
1 egg, beaten
$^{1}/_{2}$ cup fresh white bread crumbs
salt and freshly ground black pepper

1 Preheat the oven to 350°F. Cook the potatoes in a pan of boiling salted water for 20 minutes or until tender. Drain well and mash. Let cool for a few minutes. Meanwhile, melt the butter in a small pan and sauté the onion for 10 minutes, until soft.

2 Stir the butter and onion into the mashed potato and then mix in the cream and egg yolks.

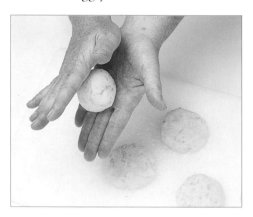

3 Sift the flour onto the potato mixture, then mix it in well. Season with plenty of salt and pepper. Shape into rounds, then flatten slightly to make about 16 "doughnuts" 2$^{1}/_{2}$ inches across.

4 Place the "doughnuts" on a lightly oiled baking sheet and brush with beaten egg. Sprinkle the tops with bread crumbs. Bake for 30 minutes or until browned.

Pampushki

When these crunchy Russian potato dumplings are split open, a tasty cottage cheese and chive filling is revealed.

INGREDIENTS

Serves 4
1½ pounds potatoes, peeled
2⅔ cups cooked mashed potatoes
½ teaspoon salt
scant ½ cup cottage cheese
2 tablespoons snipped fresh chives
freshly ground black pepper
oil, for deep-frying

1 Coarsely grate the raw potatoes and squeeze out as much water as possible. Put them in a bowl with the mashed potatoes, salt and black pepper. Combine. In another bowl, combine the cottage cheese and chives.

2 Using a spoon and your fingers, scoop up a portion of the potato mixture, slightly smaller than an egg, and then flatten to a circle.

3 Put 1 teaspoon of the cheese filling into the middle, then fold over the edges and pinch to seal. Repeat with remaining potato and cheese mixtures, to make about 12 dumplings.

4 Heat the oil to 340°F. Deep-fry the dumplings for 10 minutes or until deep brown and crisp. Drain on paper towels and serve hot.

COOK'S TIP

Pampushki are traditionally cooked in stock or water and served with soup. If you prefer to poach them, add 1 tablespoon all-purpose flour and 1 beaten egg to the mixture and poach the dumplings for 20 minutes.

Galushki

One of the most popular Ukrainian dishes, *galushki* are pieces of a pasta-like dough, cooked in milk or stock. Healthy and filling, they can be made from wheat flour, buckwheat flour, semolina or potatoes.

INGREDIENTS

Serves 4

2 cups all-purpose flour
¼ teaspoon salt
2 tablespoons butter, melted
2 eggs, beaten
1 vegetable stock cube
4 ounces bacon, chopped, to serve

1 Sift the flour and salt into a bowl. Make a well in the center. Add the butter and eggs and mix into a dough.

2 Knead on a lightly floured surface until smooth. Wrap in plastic wrap and let rest for 30 minutes. Roll out on a lightly floured surface until ½-inch thick, and cut into ¾-inch squares using a sharp knife or a pastry wheel. Let dry on a floured dish towel for 30 minutes.

3 Crumble the stock cube into a pan of gently boiling water. Add the *galushki* and simmer for 10 minutes or until cooked. Drain well.

4 Meanwhile, dry-fry the bacon in a nonstick frying pan for 5 minutes, until brown and crispy. Serve sprinkled on the *galushki*.

Cheese Dumplings

Easily prepared, dumplings are common additions to soups throughout the Ukraine. They are also served with meats and on their own as a simple supper.

INGREDIENTS

Serves 4

1 cup self-rising flour
2 tablespoons butter
⅓ cup crumbled feta, dry *brinza* (sheep's milk cheese), or a mixture of Caerphilly and Parmesan
2 tablespoons chopped fresh herbs
¼ cup cold water
salt and freshly ground black pepper
parsley sprigs, to garnish

For the topping
3 tablespoons butter
1 cup slightly dry white bread crumbs

1 Sift the flour into a bowl. Rub in the butter until the mixture resembles fine bread crumbs.

2 Stir the cheese and herbs into the mixture. Season with salt and pepper. Add the cold water and mix into a firm dough; then shape into 12 balls.

3 Bring a pan of salted water to a boil. Add the dumplings, cover and gently simmer for 20 minutes, until light and fluffy.

4 For the topping, melt the butter in a frying pan. Add the bread crumbs and cook for 2–3 minutes, until the crumbs are golden and crisp. Remove the dumplings with a slotted spoon and sprinkle with bread crumbs. Serve garnished with parsley sprigs.

Drachena

A Russian cross between an omelet and a crêpe, this is a savory *drachena,* but it is often served as a dessert by leaving out the vegetables and sweetening with sugar or honey.

INGREDIENTS

Serves 2–3

1 tablespoon olive oil
1 bunch scallions, sliced
1 garlic clove, crushed
4 tomatoes, peeled, seeded
  and chopped
3 tablespoons whole-wheat rye flour
¼ cup milk
⅔ cup sour cream
4 eggs, beaten
2 tablespoons chopped fresh parsley
2 tablespoons butter, melted
salt and freshly ground black pepper
green salad, to serve

1 Preheat the oven to 350°F. Heat the oil in a frying pan and gently cook the scallions for about 3 minutes. Add the crushed garlic clove and cook for 1 more minute or until the scallions are soft.

2 Sprinkle the scallions and garlic into the bottom of a lightly greased shallow 8-inch ovenproof dish and sprinkle on the tomatoes.

3 Mix the flour into a smooth paste in a bowl with the milk. Gradually add the sour cream, then mix with the eggs. Stir in the parsley and melted butter. Season with salt and pepper.

4 Pour the egg mixture over the vegetables. Bake for 40–45 minutes or until hardly any liquid seeps out when a knife is pushed into the middle.

5 Run a knife around the edge of the dish to loosen, then cut into wedges and serve immediately with a fresh green salad.

Braised Barley and Vegetables

One of the oldest of cultivated grains, barley has a nutty flavor and slightly chewy texture. It makes a warming and filling dish when combined with root vegetables.

INGREDIENTS

Serves 4

1 cup pearl or barley
2 tablespoons sunflower oil
1 large onion, chopped
2 celery stalks, sliced
2 carrots, halved lengthwise and sliced
8 ounces rutabaga or turnip, cut into
  ³/₄-inch cubes
8 ounces potatoes, cut into
  ³/₄-inch cubes
2 cups vegetable stock
salt and freshly ground black pepper
celery leaves, to garnish

1 Put the barley in a measuring cup and add water to reach the 2¹/₂-cup mark. Let soak in a cool place for at least 4 hours or, preferably, overnight.

2 Heat the oil in a large pan and sauté the onion for 5 minutes. Add the sliced celery and carrots and cook for 3–4 minutes, or until the onion is starting to brown.

3 Add the barley and its soaking liquid to the pan. Then add the rutabaga or turnip, potato and stock to the barley. Season with salt and pepper. Bring to a boil, then reduce the heat and cover the pan.

4 Simmer for 40 minutes, or until most of the stock has been absorbed and the barley is tender. Stir occasionally toward the end of cooking to prevent the barley from sticking to the base of the pan. Serve, garnished with celery leaves.

Beet Casserole

This Russian vegetarian casserole can be served as a light meal in itself. Its sweet and sour flavor also makes it an ideal dish to serve with roasted chicken or game.

INGREDIENTS

Serves 4

¹/₄ cup butter
1 onion, chopped
2 garlic cloves, crushed
1½ pounds uncooked beets, peeled
2 large carrots, peeled
½ lemon
1½ cups button mushrooms
1¼ cups vegetable stock
2 bay leaves
1 tablespoon chopped fresh mint, plus
   sprigs to garnish (optional)
salt and freshly ground black pepper

For the hot dressing

²/₃ cup sour cream
½ teaspoon paprika, plus extra
   to garnish

1 Melt the butter in a non–aluminum pan and gently sauté the onion and garlic for 5 minutes. Meanwhile, dice the beets and carrot. Finely grate the zest and squeeze the juice of the ½ lemon. Add the beets, carrots and mushrooms and cook for 5 minutes.

——— COOK'S TIP ———

Wear clean rubber or plastic gloves to avoid staining your hands when preparing beet-root. Cooking beets in aluminum pans may cause discoloration of pan and food.

2 Pour in the stock with the lemon zest and bay leaves. Season with salt and pepper. Bring to a boil, turn down the heat, cover and simmer for 1 hour, or until the vegetables are soft.

3 Turn off the heat and stir in the lemon juice and chopped mint, if using. Let the pan stand, covered, for 5 minutes, to develop the flavors.

4 Meanwhile, for the dressing, gently heat the sour cream and paprika in a small pan, stirring all the time, until bubbling. Transfer the beets mixture to a serving bowl, then spoon over the sour cream. Garnish with sprigs of mint and extra paprika, if desired, and serve.

Uszka

Uszka, meaning "little ears," are plump mushroom dumplings, traditionally served in Poland with clear soups. They are also delicious on their own, tossed in a little melted butter and chopped fresh herbs.

INGREDIENTS

Makes 20

²/₃ cup all-purpose flour
pinch of salt
2 tablespoons chopped fresh parsley
1 egg yolk
2¹/₂ tablespoons cold water
fresh parsley, to garnish
clear soup or melted herb butter,
   to serve

For the filling

2 tablespoons butter
¹/₂ small onion, very finely chopped
1 cup mushrooms, finely chopped
1 egg white
1 tablespoon dry white bread crumbs
salt and freshly ground black pepper

1 Sift the flour and salt into a bowl. Add the chopped parsley, egg yolk and water and mix to a dough. Lightly knead the dough on a floured surface until smooth.

2 To make the filling, melt the butter in a pan. Add the onion and mushrooms and sauté over low heat for 10 minutes or until the onion is very soft. Let cool.

3 Lightly whisk the egg white in a clean bowl with a fork. Add 1 tablespoon of the egg white to the mushrooms, together with the bread crumbs, salt and pepper. Combine well.

4 Roll out the dough very thinly on a floured surface. Cut into 2-inch squares using a sharp knife or a pastry wheel, then lightly brush with the remaining egg white.

5 Spoon ¹/₂ teaspoon of mushroom mixture on each square. Fold the dough in half to make a triangle, then pinch the outer edges together to seal them.

6 Bring a pan of boiling salted water or stock to a brisk boil. Gently drop in the dumplings a few at a time and simmer for 5 minutes. Drain and add to a clear soup or toss in melted herb butter and serve.

Cucumber Salad

Salting the cucumber draws out some of the moisture, thereby making it firmer. Make sure you rinse it thoroughly before using or the salad will be too salty. This popular Ukrainian dish is an ideal accompaniment to a main course.

INGREDIENTS

Serves 6–8
2 cucumbers, decorated with a
    cannelle knife and thinly sliced
1 teaspoon salt
3 tablespoons chopped fresh dill
1 tablespoon white wine vinegar
²/₃ cup sour cream
freshly ground black pepper
1 dill sprig, to garnish

1 Put the cucumber in a sieve or colander set over a bowl and sprinkle with the salt. Set aside for 1 hour to drain. Rinse the cucumber well under cold running water, then pat dry with paper towels.

2 Put the slices of cucumber in a bowl, add the chopped dill and combine everything well.

3 In another bowl, stir the vinegar into the sour cream and season the mixture with pepper.

4 Pour the sour cream over the cucumber and chill for 1 hour before turning into a serving dish. Garnish with a sprig of dill and serve.

Grated Beet and Celery Salad

Raw beets have an appealing texture. Here, in this Russian salad, their flavor is brought out by marinating in a cider dressing.

INGREDIENTS

Serves 4–6
1 pound uncooked beets, peeled
    and grated
4 celery stalks, finely chopped
2 tablespoons apple juice
fresh herbs, to garnish

For the dressing
3 tablespoons sunflower oil
1 tablespoon cider vinegar
4 scallions, finely sliced
2 tablespoons chopped fresh parsley
salt and freshly ground black pepper

1 Toss the beets, celery and apple juice together in a bowl to mix.

2 Put all the ingredients for the dressing in a small bowl and whisk with a fork until well blended. Stir half into the beet mixture.

3 Drizzle the remaining dressing on top. Let the salad marinate for at least 2 hours before serving, for the fullest flavor. Garnish with fresh herbs.

DESSERTS & BAKED GOODS

Russians, Ukrainians and Poles often have a sweet tooth, and this is reflected in their vast numbers and varieties of desserts, cakes, pastries and breads. Special occasions are often marked with particular confections, such as Russian Paskha and Polish Babka. Honey and nuts are plentiful and feature in many sweet dishes. Other popular flavorings are cinnamon, cloves and cardamom, as well as candied fruits, vanilla and lemon peel. Fruit, especially orchard fruits and berries, can be of exceptionally high quality.

Polish Honey Cake

Many Eastern European cakes, like this Polish *Tort Orzechowy*, are sweetened with honey and made with ground nuts and bread crumbs instead of flour, which gives them a delicious, rich, moist texture.

INGREDIENTS

Serves 12

1 tablespoon unsalted butter, melted and cooled
2 cups slightly dry fine white bread crumbs
³/₄ cup honey, plus extra to serve
¹/₄ cup light brown sugar
4 eggs, separated
1 cup hazelnuts, chopped and toasted, plus extra to decorate

1 Preheat the oven to 350°F. Brush a 7¹/₂-cup fluted brioche pan with the melted butter. Sprinkle with ¹/₄ cup of the bread crumbs.

—— COOK'S TIP ——

The cake will rise during cooking and sink slightly as it cools—this is quite normal.

2 Put the honey in a large bowl, set over a pan of barely simmering water. When the honey liquifies, add the sugar and egg yolks. Whisk until light and frothy. Remove from heat.

3 Mix the remaining bread crumbs with the hazelnuts and fold into the egg yolk and honey mixture. Whisk the egg whites in a separate bowl, until stiff, then gently fold in to the other ingredients, half at a time.

4 Spoon the mixture into the pan. Bake for 40–45 minutes, until golden brown. Let cool in the pan for 5 minutes, then turn out onto a wire rack to cool. Sprinkle on nuts and drizzle with extra honey to serve.

Baked Coffee Custards

Unlike the Russians and Ukrainians, the Polish have a passion for coffee and use it in many of their desserts.

INGREDIENTS

Serves 4

6 tablespoons finely ground coffee
1¼ cups milk
⅔ cup light cream
2 eggs, beaten
2 tablespoons sugar
whipped cream and unsweetened cocoa powder, to decorate

1 Preheat the oven to 375°F. Put the ground coffee in a bowl. Heat the milk in a pan until it is almost boiling. Pour in with the coffee and let stand for 5 minutes.

2 Strain the coffee-flavored milk back into the pan. Add the cream and heat again until almost boiling.

3 Beat the eggs and sugar in a bowl. Pour the hot coffee-flavored milk into the bowl, whisking constantly. Strain into the rinsed bowl.

4 Pour the mixture into 4 × ⅔-cup ramekins. Cover each with a piece of aluminum foil.

5 Put the ramekins in a roasting pan and pour in enough hot water to come halfway up the sides of the ramekins. Bake for 40 minutes or until lightly set.

6 Remove the ramekins from the roasting pan and let cool. Chill for 2 hours. Decorate with a swirl of whipped cream and a sprinkle of cocoa powder, if desired, before serving.

Tort Migdalowy

Almonds are in plentiful supply in Poland and are used in both sweet and savory dishes. Here they are roasted, giving this coffee-cream-filled cake a rich and nutty flavor.

INGREDIENTS

Serves 8–10
½ cup blanched almonds
1 cup butter, softened
generous 1 cup sugar
4 eggs, beaten
1¼ cups self-rising flour, sifted

For the icing

1 cup blanched almonds
9 tablespoons ground coffee
5 tablespoons almost-boiling water
¾ cup sugar
6 tablespoons water
3 egg yolks
1 cup unsalted butter

1 Preheat the oven to 375°F. Lightly grease and line 3 × 7-inch round cake pans with waxed paper.

2 Put the blanched almonds on a baking sheet and roast for 7 minutes or until golden brown.

3 Let cool, then transfer to a processor or a blender and process until fine.

4 Cream the butter and sugar together in a bowl until pale and fluffy. Gradually add the eggs, a little at a time, beating well after each addition. Fold in the ground roasted almonds and the flour.

5 Divide the cake mixture evenly between the 3 prepared pans and bake for 25–30 minutes, until well risen and firm to the touch, switching the position of the top and bottom cakes halfway through cooking. Turn out and cool on a wire rack.

6 For the icing, put the blanched almonds in a bowl and pour in enough boiling water to cover. Set aside until cold, then drain the almonds and cut each one lengthwise into 4 or 5 slivers with a sharp knife. Roast on a baking sheet for 6–8 minutes.

7 Put the ground coffee in a bowl, add the water and let stand. Gently heat the sugar and 6 tablespoons water in a small heavy pan until dissolved. Simmer for 3 minutes, until the temperature reaches 225°F on a sugar thermometer.

8 Put the egg yolks into a bowl and pour in the syrup in a thin stream, whisking constantly until very thick. Cream the butter until soft, then gradually beat the egg mixture into it.

9 Strain the coffee through a sieve and beat into the icing. Use two-thirds to sandwich the cakes together. Spread the remainder on top and press in the almond slivers.

Raisin Cheesecake

Cheesecakes were originally baked rather than set with gelatin. This Ukrainian dessert is an Easter specialty.

INGREDIENTS

Serves 8

1 cup all-purpose flour
1/4 cup butter
1 tablespoon sugar
1/4 cup almonds, very finely chopped
2 tablespoons cold water
1 tablespoon confectioners' sugar,
　for dusting

For the filling

8 tablespoons butter
3/4 cup sugar
1 teaspoon vanilla extract
3 eggs, beaten
1/4 cup all-purpose flour, sifted
1 3/4 cups ricotta cheese
grated zest and juice of 2 lemons
1/2 cup raisins

1 Sift the flour into a bowl. Rub in the butter, until the mixture resembles fine bread crumbs. Stir in the sugar and almonds. Add the water and mix into a dough. Lightly knead on a floured surface for a few seconds. Wrap in plastic wrap and chill for 30 minutes.

2 Preheat the oven to 400°F. Roll out the pastry on a lightly floured surface to a 10-inch circle and use it to line the bottom and sides of an 8-inch tart pan. Trim the edges of the pastry with a sharp knife.

3 Prick with a fork, cover with oiled aluminum foil and bake for 6 minutes. Remove the foil and bake for 6 more minutes. Let cool and reduce the temperature to 300°F.

4 For the filling, cream the butter, sugar and vanilla together. Beat in one egg, then stir in the flour. Beat the cheese until soft, then gradually mix in the remaining eggs. Blend this into the butter mixture. Stir in the lemon zest, juice and raisins.

5 Pour the filling onto the pastry crust. Bake for 1 1/2 hours, until firm. Turn off the oven, leave the door ajar and let cool before removing. Dust with confectioners' sugar.

Polish Crêpes

Fluffy crêpes are filled with a cheese and golden raisin mixture.

INGREDIENTS

Makes 6
1 cup all-purpose flour
pinch of salt
pinch of grated nutmeg, plus extra
   for dusting
1 egg, separated
scant 1 cup milk
2 tablespoons sunflower oil
2 tablespoons butter
lemon slices, to garnish

For the filling
1 cup ricotta cheese
1 tablespoon sugar
1 teaspoon vanilla extract
scant ½ cup golden raisins

1 Sift the flour, salt and nutmeg together in a large bowl. Make a well in the center. Add the yolk and half of the milk. Beat until smooth, then gradually beat in the remaining milk.

2 Whisk the egg white in a bowl until stiff. Fold into the batter.

3 Heat 1 teaspoon sunflower oil and a little of the butter in a 7-inch frying pan. Pour in enough of the batter to cover the bottom.

4 Cook for 2 minutes, until golden brown, then turn over and cook for another 2 minutes.

5 Make 5 more crêpes in the same way, using more oil and butter as necessary. Stack up the crêpes and keep them warm.

6 To make the filling, put the ricotta cheese, sugar and vanilla in a bowl and beat together. Mix in the golden raisins. Divide among the crêpes, fold them up and dust with grated nutmeg. Garnish with lemon slices.

Apricot Treat

Fresh fruit was once scarce in Poland during winter, so dried fruits were often used. This rich apricot and almond dessert, a favorite in Poland, resembles the desserts more common to the Balkan regions.

INGREDIENTS

Serves 6

1 cup dried apricots, chopped
3 tablespoons water
¼ cup sugar
½ cup chopped almonds
⅓ cup chopped candied orange peel
confectioners' sugar, for dusting
whipped cream, to serve
ground cinnamon, to decorate

1 Put the apricots and water in a heavy pan. Cover and simmer, stirring, for about 20 minutes, until a thick paste forms.

2 Stir in the sugar and simmer, stirring, for another 10 minutes, until quite dry. Remove from heat and stir in the almonds and chopped orange peel.

3 Using a knife, shape into a "sausage," about 2-inches thick, on a piece of waxed paper dusted with confectioners' sugar.

4 Let dry in a cool place for at least 3 hours. Cut into slices and serve with whipped cream, sprinkled with a little cinnamon.

Dried Fruit Compote

Fruit grows in abundance in orchards throughout the Ukraine and dried fruits are used all year round. *Uzvar* is served on Christmas Eve and also at feasts at which the dead are honored. This easy and delicious dessert is also made in Russia.

INGREDIENTS

Serves 6

2 cups mixed dried fruits, such as apples, pears, prunes, peaches or apricots
1 cinnamon stick
1¼ cups cider or water
½ cup raisins
2 tablespoons honey
juice of ½ lemon
mint leaves, to decorate

1 Put the mixed dried fruit in a large pan with the cinnamon and cider or water. Heat gently until almost boiling, then cover the pan, lower the heat and cook gently for 12–15 minutes, to soften the fruit.

— COOK'S TIP —

This compote will keep refrigerated for up to a week.

2 Remove the pan from heat and stir in the raisins and honey. Cover the pan and let cool. Remove the cinnamon stick and then stir in the lemon juice.

3 Transfer the compote to a serving bowl, cover with plastic wrap and keep refrigerated until needed. Let the fruit compote come to room temperature before serving, decorated with a few mint leaves.

Plum and Almond Tart

Plums and almonds have a natural affinity, and this Russian tart with its simple pastry crust is a great way to serve them. Serve with homemade custard.

INGREDIENTS

Serves 6
1½ cups all-purpose flour
8 tablespoons butter, chilled
¼ cup sour cream

For the topping
¼ cup butter, softened
¼ cup sugar, plus 2 tablespoons
   for sprinkling
2 eggs, beaten
1 cup ground almonds
about 6 plums, quartered and pitted
scant ½ cup plum jam
¼ cup sliced almonds

1 Sift the flour into a mixing bowl. Dice the butter and rub in until the mixture resembles fine bread crumbs. Stir in the sour cream to make a soft dough. Wrap in plastic wrap and chill for at least 30 minutes.

COOK'S TIP

Apricots can be used instead of plums, as an alternative, if desired.

2 For the topping, cream the butter and sugar until light. Add the eggs, alternating with the ground almonds.

3 Preheat the oven to 425°F. Roll out the pastry on a lightly floured surface into a 12-inch round, then transfer to a large baking sheet. Prick all over.

4 Spread the almond mixture on the pastry, leaving a border of about 1½ inches. Arrange the plums on top. Sprinkle with the 2 tablespoons of sugar. Turn in the border.

5 Bake the tart for 35–40 minutes or until browned. Warm the plum jam in a small pan, press through a sieve and brush on the tart to glaze. Sprinkle almonds on top to decorate.

VARIATION

The recipe could be used to make 4 individual tarts, like the one shown here. Thickly slice the plums instead of cutting them into quarters. Finish the tarts as above with the jam glaze and almonds.

Lepeshki

With characteristic Russian preference for all things sour, these cookies are made with sour cream instead of butter.

INGREDIENTS

Makes 24
2 cups self-rising flour
pinch of salt
1/2 cup sugar
1 egg, separated
1/2 cup sour cream
1/2 teaspoon each vanilla and
    almond extract
1 tablespoon milk
1/2 cup sliced almonds

1 Preheat the oven to 400°F. Sift the flour, salt and sugar into a mixing bowl and make a well in the center.

2 Reserve 2 teaspoons of the egg white. Mix the remainder with the egg yolk, sour cream, vanilla and almond extracts and milk. Add to the dry ingredients and mix to form a soft dough.

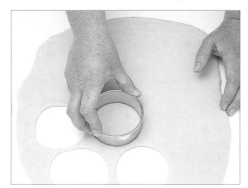

3 Roll out the dough on a lightly floured surface until about 1/3 inch thick, then stamp out rounds with a 3-inch cutter.

4 Transfer the circles to lightly oiled baking sheets. Brush with the reserved egg white and sprinkle with the sliced almonds.

5 Bake for 10 minutes, until light golden brown. Transfer to a wire rack and let cool. Store the cookies in an airtight container.

Babka

A typical Polish Easter menu is a grand affair and may include a roast suckling pig, brightly colored eggs and *Babka*—the word means "Grandmother." The cake was so named because it is made with gentleness and loving care.

INGREDIENTS

Serves 8
3 cups all-purpose flour
½ teaspoon salt
2 tablespoons sugar
1 teaspoon active dry yeast
8 tablespoons butter, softened
⅔ cup warm milk
4 egg yolks
scant 1 cup golden raisins
finely grated zest of 1 orange
¼ cup honey, warmed
butter, to serve

1 Sift the flour, salt and sugar into a large bowl. Stir in the yeast, then make a well in the center.

2 Add the butter, milk, egg yolks, dried fruit and orange zest. Mix into a dough. Turn out on a lightly floured surface and knead for 10 minutes, until smooth and elastic.

3 Put the dough in a well-greased 2½-pound fluted cake pan. Cover with oiled plastic wrap and set in a warm place to rise for 1 hour or until doubled in size.

4 Preheat the oven to 375°F. Bake for 45–50 minutes or until firm and a skewer inserted into the middle comes out clean.

5 Let the cake cool in the pan for 5 minutes. Turn out onto a wire rack and brush all over with the warmed honey. When cold, slice thickly and serve with butter.

Christmas Cookies

These spiced cookies may be used as edible decorations: thread them with colored ribbon and hang on the branches of the Christmas tree, as is traditionally done in the Ukraine.

INGREDIENTS

Makes 30
¼ cup butter
1 tablespoon light corn syrup
   or honey
¼ cup light brown sugar
2 cups all-purpose flour
2 teaspoons ground cinnamon
1 teaspoon ground ginger
¼ teaspoon grated nutmeg
½ teaspoon baking soda
3 tablespoons milk
1 egg yolk
2 tablespoons sugar sprinkles

1 Preheat the oven to 350°F. Line 2 baking sheets with baking parchment. Melt the butter, syrup or honey and brown sugar in a pan. Let cool for 5 minutes.

2 Sift the flour, cinnamon, ginger, nutmeg and baking soda into a bowl. Make a well in the center. Pour in the melted butter mixture, milk and egg yolk. Mix into a soft dough.

3 Knead until smooth, then roll out between 2 sheets of baking parchment until ¼ inch thick. Stamp out shapes using cookie cutters.

--- COOK'S TIP ---

Roll out the dough while it is still warm, since it becomes hard and brittle as it cools.

4 Place on the baking sheets. Make a hole in each with a skewer if you want to hang them up later. Sprinkle with colored sugar sprinkles. Bake for 10 minutes, until a slightly darker shade. Cool slightly, then transfer to a wire rack and let cool completely.

Sour Rye Bread

Traditionally, the "starter" would be a little dough left over from a previous bread-making session, but it's simple to make your own. The starter gives this bread its delicious, slightly sour taste.

INGREDIENTS

Makes 2 loaves

4 cups rye flour, plus extra for dusting (optional)

4 cups all-purpose flour

1 tablespoon salt

¼-ounce envelope active dry yeast

2 tablespoons butter, softened

2½ cups warm water

1 tablespoon caraway seeds or buckwheat, for sprinkling (optional)

For the sourdough starter

¼ cup rye flour

3 tablespoons warm milk

1 For the starter, combine the rye flour and milk in a small bowl. Cover with plastic wrap and set aside in a warm place for 1–2 days or until it smells pleasantly sour.

2 To make the loaves, sift together the flour and salt into a large bowl. Next, stir in the yeast. Make a well in the center and add the butter, water and sourdough starter already prepared. With a wooden spoon, mix well until you have a soft dough.

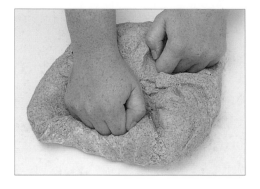

3 Turn out the dough onto a lightly floured surface and knead for 10 minutes, until smooth and elastic. Put in a clean bowl, cover with plastic wrap and set aside in a warm place to rise for 1 hour or until doubled in size.

4 Knead for 1 minute, then divide the dough in half. Shape each piece into a round 6 inches across. Transfer to 2 greased baking sheets. Cover with oiled plastic wrap and let rise for 30 minutes.

5 Preheat the oven to 400°F. Brush the loaves with water, then sprinkle with caraway seeds or buckwheat, or dust with rye flour.

6 Bake for 35–40 minutes or until the loaves are browned and sound hollow when tapped on the bottom. Cool on a wire rack.

COOK'S TIP

Sour rye bread keeps fresh for up to a week. This recipe can also be made without yeast, but it will be much denser.

Poppy Seed Roll

This sweet bread with its spiral filling of dried fruits and poppy seeds, is a wonderful example of traditional Polish cooking and is a favorite. The seeds have a gritty texture and keep the cake moist.

INGREDIENTS

Serves 12
4 cups all-purpose flour
pinch of salt
2 tablespoons sugar
2 teaspoons active dry yeast
³/₄ cup milk
finely grated zest of 1 lemon
¹/₄ cup butter

For the filling and glaze
¹/₄ cup butter
²/₃ cup poppy seeds
¹/₄ cup honey
¹/₂ cup raisins
scant ¹/₂ cup finely chopped candied
   orange peel
¹/₂ cup ground almonds
1 egg yolk
¹/₄ cup sugar
1 tablespoon milk
¹/₄ cup apricot jam
1 tablespoon lemon juice
1 tablespoon rum or brandy
¹/₄ cup toasted sliced almonds

1 Sift the flour, salt and sugar into a bowl. Stir in the yeast. Make a well in the center.

2 Heat the milk and lemon zest in a pan with the butter, until melted. Cool a little, then add to the dry ingredients and mix into a dough.

3 Knead the dough on a lightly floured surface for 10 minutes, until smooth and elastic. Put in a clean bowl, cover and set in a warm place to rise for 45–50 minutes or until doubled in size.

4 For the filling, melt the butter in a pan. Reserve 1 tablespoon of poppy seeds, then process the rest and add to the pan with the honey, raisins and peel. Cook gently for 5 minutes. Stir in the almonds; let cool.

5 Whisk the egg yolk and sugar together in a bowl until pale, then fold into the poppy seed mixture. Roll out the dough on a lightly floured surface into a 12 × 14-inch rectangle. Spread the filling to within 1-inch of the edges.

6 Roll both ends toward the center. Cover with oiled plastic wrap and let rise for 30 minutes. Preheat the oven to 375°F.

7 Brush with the milk, then sprinkle with the reserved poppy seeds. Bake for 30 minutes, until golden brown.

8 Heat the jam and lemon juice gently until bubbling. Sieve, then stir in the rum or brandy. Brush onto the roll while still warm and sprinkle the almonds on top.

GERMANY, AUSTRIA, HUNGARY AND THE CZECH REPUBLIC

Drawing on influences from Russia, France and Turkey, the cooking of this area is famous for its filling stews and dumplings, distinctive use of ingredients such as sauerkraut and paprika, and excellence in cake and pastry making.

INTRODUCTION

The Central European countries of Germany, Austria, Hungary, the Czech Republic and Slovakia comprise a geographical region that extends southward from the cold shores of the North and Baltic Seas to the warmer climes of the Balkan countries. The foods characteristic of this area thus reflect a wide range of influences, though they are characterized by a robust style that is famous worldwide.

CULINARY IDENTITY
On an everyday level of eating and drinking, national tastes within Central Europe have tended to remain simple and relatively distinct. The wide availability of many typical ingredients, however, such as caraway seeds, cucumbers, dill, mustard, sour cream and cabbage, has naturally resulted in an overlap of cooking styles, and

sometimes recipes of neighboring countries may vary only slightly in ingredients or method.

Czech cooking, for example, is solid and satisfying and bland in flavor except for the use of marjoram. Pale rye bread is preferred, as are salads of potatoes and other cooked vegetables, often dressed with mayonnaise. Potatoes are also fried with bacon or simmered with sausage to make quickly prepared supper dishes. Much use is made of other root crops, such as kohlrabi and celeriac. The best loved of all Czech dishes, however, has to be the dumpling. Made of flour, semolina or potato, in all shapes and sizes, these are served in savory soups and stews as well as desserts.

In contrast with such mild flavors and hefty textures, Hungarian cooking can be quite fiery and is

rich in Mediterranean-style vegetables. The sour flavors and pickles that are so characteristic of the rest of Eastern Europe are less often seen in Hungarian cooking. The abundance of wheat ensures plenty of robust white bread, instead of darker breads, and more use of homemade pasta.

HUNGARIAN FINESSE
In the best of Hungarian cooking, as in some German cuisine, the use of red and white wine in meat and fish dishes has produced a greater complexity and subtlety than in other Central European cuisines, establishing a dividing line between good Hungarian cooking and the more usual country-style fare of the region. Hungarian chefs also have different ways of cooking meat and fish with paprika, according to whether or not the finished dish is

Left: The following collection of recipes concentrates on the Central European countries, where hearty peasant traditions sit alongside the opulence of dishes that flourished during the period of the great Austro-Hungarian Hapsburg Empire.

Right: Fresh produce available at the markets ranges from root vegetables characteristic of northern Europe to tomatoes, zucchini and bell peppers, more typical of the warmer southern cuisines.

dry or whether it contains cream. Goulash itself is always a dish with plenty of sauce.

It appears that the development of such fine Hungarian cuisine and the adoption of a wide variety of ingredients, including tomatoes, onions and peppers, was a consequence of an important royal marriage in the 15th century. In 1475, King Matthias married the daughter of the King of Naples, who imported new ingredients and chefs to make life beyond Italy's borders bearable. From these early refinements, Hungarian cuisine has rarely looked back.

MEAT DISHES
A key ingredient of this region's cooking is pork. Although the world-famous Austrian schnitzel is usually made with veal, across Germany and the other Central European countries, pork is more commonly eaten, either as fried steaks or cooked with peppers. In the Czech Republic, it is also served wrapped around an egg, ham and cheese filling. It is also often stewed, as a variation on the classic Hungarian goulash.

Cured pork, or bacon, is another important ingredient in Central European cooking, valued for its unique pervasive flavor. Czech and Hungarian cooks, for example, use bacon fat to achieve the distinctive taste of many soups and otherwise meat-free fare, including dishes of long-simmered red cabbage.

Pork is also the major ingredient of the region's sausages. Czech sausages and Hungarian salami are famous worldwide, and every German region has its distinctive *wurst*, or sausage.

Beef perhaps rivals pork in popularity only in those parts of Central Eastern Europe where the best cattle are raised. One such

place is the central Hungarian plain, or *puszta*, the original home of goulash, which is named after the *gulyás* (cowherds) who invented the prototype dish. While today's tempting recipes for this classic dish make use of paprika, caraway, green bell peppers and tomatoes, the cowherds of past centuries simply added water to meat they had previously cooked with onions, then dried in the sun.

Although they have no such romantic history, German beef dishes are also excellent: for example, recipes for *sauerbraten*, beef marinated in vinegar, sugar and seasonings, then braised, simply show off high-quality beef at its best.

JEWISH HERITAGE
Much of Central and Eastern European cuisine is known to the West in the guise of Jewish cooking, dating from the time when many Jewish communities inhabited this part of Europe. Czech and traditional Jewish cooking, for instance, share a taste for goose and beef, as well as for carp served in sweetish sauces. Jewish *gefilte fish*, carp stuffed with

pike, uses two of the classic fish of the region. Pancakes, beans and fried cakes of grated raw potato figure in both cuisines. The Jewish Sabbath dish of *cholent*, bean and barley stew, is simply a kosher variation of the pork versions of the dish found everywhere in Central Europe. By the same token, Jewish recipes for red cabbage dispense with bacon.

CAKES AND PASTRIES
The fine tradition of cakes and pastries common to southern Germany, Austria and Hungary owes much to the bread and pastry cooks of 18th-century Vienna, who in turn were inspired by a mixture of French and Turkish influences. German, Austro-Hungarian and Jewish cakemakers of the past two and a half centuries have together created the greatest tortes and strudels in the world, and the most civilized surroundings in which to eat them while drinking coffee.

While the range of cakes available is great, a good plain cake that straddles all borders is the *gugelhupf* or *kugelhupf*. This is leavened with yeast and traditionally baked in a Turk's head mold.

INGREDIENTS

VEGETABLES

Fresh red and green bell peppers of the large capsicum variety, tomatoes and zucchini, parsley and dill are among the abundant vegetables and fresh herbs you would expect to see in a Hungarian market. In addition to large onions for cooking, scallions are used in salads and to garnish soups. The more unusual root crops in Germany and the Czech lands include kohlrabi, a relative of the cabbage family, and celeriac, a large bumpy root vegetable, which can be used in soups or salads.

MEAT AND POULTRY

Fresh pork is the most popular meat, with goose cooked for special occasions. Central European food is most famous, however, for its smoked and unsmoked pork sausage and bacon. Bacon teams particularly well with cabbage and

caraway, and bacon fat is often used to enhance the flavor of soups and stews. As for sausages, from Germany through the Czech Republic to Slovakia and Hungary, these are eternally popular street food, eaten simply with mustard and a roll, and they double as quick meals in pubs and restaurants. The number of varieties available at shops and delicatessens, from the frankfurter style to juicy fat specimens, can easily overwhelm the uninitiated. The range of salami-style sausage, which in German is called *wurst*, is equally wide and delicious.

GRAINS

Central Europe is the home of *mehlspeisen*, dishes of noodles or dumplings, which can be either sweet or savory and take the place of a meat-based course. Dumplings are made of flour and semolina and sometimes include potato. Good white flour is essential for fine baking, and excellent white bread is produced alongside traditional pale rye bread.

HERBS, SPICES AND OTHER FLAVORINGS

Paprika was introduced to daily Hungarian cooking by the Turks some time before the 17th century, but it took a long time before the upper classes adopted the habit. To make paprika powder, the fleshy parts of peppers are dried and powdered, with a proportion of their seeds. The result is graded according to piquancy, fineness and color, with the colors varying from bright red to yellowish brown. "Sweet noble" paprika is darker and more piquant than the duller,

Above left: capsicum, tomatoes, celeriac, onions and kohlrabi.

Above right: assorted German breads, including sourdough, pumpernickel, rye and poppy seed.

Right, clockwise from front left: smoked loin, Hungarian guylai, *pork medallion steaks, boned shoulder, pork ribs,* bauernbratwurst, regensburgers *and* frankfurters.

Above, counterclockwise from left: apples, plums, cherries, hazelnuts and almonds

Left, from left to right: dried chiles, paprika and fresh and bottled chiles

lighter, half-sweet paprika, which can give good color to a dish without making it unbearably hot. Many Hungarian dishes are begun by lightly frying an onion and sprinkling some paprika powder on it.

Caraway seed, which has a cooling and digestive effect, is widely used in cabbage dishes and with pork. The flowery, pungent taste of fresh marjoram, which retains its flavor uniquely well among herbs when dried, is a year-round favorite with Czech cooks. Mustard of a mild European variety is the essential accompaniment to the boiled sausages of Central East Europe.

In baking, honey, poppy seeds and cake spices, such as cinnamon, cloves and cardamom, are used to flavor traditional sweet cookies and breads, including gingerbread and braided buns.

Right, clockwise from left: fresh marjoram; plain, dill and whole-grain mustards; cardamom; cinnamon sticks; poppy seeds; caraway seeds and allspice.

FRUIT

The plums, apricots and cherries of Central Europe make outstanding jams and pie fillings. Apples are widely used and are delicious with braised red cabbage. Germany is one of the largest apple-growing countries in the world, and there is seemingly no limit to the guises in which apples can appear, from strudels and pancakes to cakes.

DAIRY PRODUCTS

Hungarian *lipto* cheese is a specialty sheep's milk cheese, and is the chief ingredient in *liptauer,* a spread made with butter, paprika, caraway and onion. Cottage and ricotta cheeses are used in savory and sweet dishes.

DRINKS

Czech beer from Pilsen is arguably the finest in the world. Whatever the country of origin, German lager-style beer is enjoyed throughout Central Eastern Europe and is sometimes used in cooking.

Modest white table wines are produced in Moravia and Slovakia, but the best wine comes from Hungary, from around Lake Balaton and a little further north in the prized Badacsonyi region, and also in the south in Villany, close to Croatia and Serbia. Hungary is also famous for its very sweet dessert wine called *tokai,* produced in a small area in the north of the country, straddling the border with Slovakia. It may be drunk at both the beginning and end of a meal, or added to consommé.

Each Central European country has its favorite brandy or what the Germans call schnapps. One well-known example is the Hungarian *palinka,* made out of apricots. *Slivowicz,* made from plums, is common everywhere. A Czech specialty is a sweetish herbal liqueur called *bekerovka.*

SOUPS AND APPETIZERS

Soups are a favorite in this area, served either as a main course or as an appetizer. Hearty soups range from creamy dishes such as Czech Cauliflower Soup accompanied by light dumplings, to the famous fruit soups of Hungary and chunky soups of Germany, such as Lentil Soup containing sliced frankfurters. Many Central European starters consist of sour vegetables, cold meats, fish and cheese. Served hot or cold, tasty appetizers such as Potato Pancakes and Herbed Liver Pâté Pie are ideal as snacks to serve with drinks.

Cream of Spinach Soup

Rich and smooth, Hungarian creamed soups are made with heavy or sour cream and sometimes egg yolk, too.

INGREDIENTS

Serves 4

1¼ pounds fresh young spinach, well washed
5 cups salted water
2 onions, very finely chopped or minced
2 tablespoons butter
3 tablespoons all-purpose flour
1 cup heavy cream
salt and freshly ground black pepper
2 hard-boiled eggs, sliced, and 2 strips bacon, crumbled, to garnish

1 Remove and discard any coarse stems from the spinach leaves. Bring the salted water to a boil. in a large pan. Add the spinach and cook for 5–6 minutes. Strain the spinach and reserve the liquid.

2 Blend the spinach in a food processor or blender into a purée.

3 Sauté the chopped or minced onions in the butter in a large pan until pale golden brown. Remove from heat and sprinkle in the flour. Return to the heat and cook for another 1–2 minutes to cook the flour.

4 Stir in the reserved spinach liquid and, once it is all incorporated into the soup, bring it back to a boil.

5 Cook until thick, then stir in the spinach purée and heavy cream. Reheat and adjust the seasoning. Serve the soup in bowls garnished with extra pepper, and the sliced eggs and sprinkled with the crumbled bacon pieces.

Lentil Soup

This is a wonderfully hearty German *Linsensuppe*, but a lighter version can be made by omitting the frankfurters, if preferred.

INGREDIENTS

Serves 6

1 cup brown lentils
1 tablespoon sunflower oil
1 onion, finely chopped
1 leek, finely chopped
1 carrot, finely diced
2 celery stalks, chopped
4-ounce piece of bacon
2 bay leaves
6¼ cups water
2 tablespoons chopped fresh parsley, plus extra to garnish
8 ounces frankfurters, sliced
salt and freshly ground black pepper

1 Rinse the lentils thoroughly under cold running water.

2 Heat the oil in a large pan and gently sauté the onion for 5 minutes, until soft. Add the leek, carrot, celery, bacon and bay leaves.

3 Add the lentils. Pour in the water, then slowly bring to a boil. Skim the surface then simmer, half-covered, for 45–50 minutes, or until the lentils are soft.

4 Remove the piece of bacon from the soup and cut into small cubes. Trim off any excess fat.

5 Return to the soup with the parsley and sliced frankfurters, and season with salt and pepper. Simmer for 2–3 minutes, remove the bay leaves, and serve garnished with the parsley.

--- COOK'S TIP ---

Unlike most pulses, brown lentils do not need to be soaked before cooking.

Cauliflower Soup

This puréed soup has the smooth texture typical of Czech soups.

INGREDIENTS

Serves 6–8

1 large cauliflower, cut into florets
6¼ cups water or chicken stock
3 tablespoons butter
⅓ cup all-purpose flour
generous pinch of nutmeg or mace
2 egg yolks
1¼ cups whipping cream
flat-leaf parsley, to garnish
crusty bread, to serve

For the dumplings

1½ cups white bread crumbs
½ tablespoon butter, softened
1 egg, beaten
2 teaspoons chopped fresh parsley
a little milk, to bind
salt and freshly ground black pepper

1 Cook the cauliflower in the water or chicken stock for 12 minutes or until just tender. Remove and reserve the cooking liquid and a few florets of the cauliflower.

2 Make a sauce by melting the butter in a small pan. Add the flour and cook for 1–2 minutes, before adding about ⅔ cup of the reserved cauliflower cooking liquid and stirring well. Remove from heat.

3 Purée the cooked cauliflower in a food processor or blender until smooth. Beat the nutmeg or mace and egg yolks into the cauliflower, then add to the pan of sauce.

4 Add enough cauliflower liquid to make up to 5 cups. Reheat the soup.

5 Make the dumplings by mixing all the ingredients together. Roll into firm small balls.

6 Poach the dumplings gently in the soup for 3–5 minutes before adding the whipping cream. Garnish with sprigs of flat-leaf parsley and the reserved cauliflower and serve with crusty bread.

Fish Soup with Dumplings

This Czech soup takes little time to make compared with a meat-based one. Use a variety of whatever fish is available, such as perch, catfish, cod, snapper or carp. The basis of the dumplings is the same whether you use semolina or all-purpose flour.

INGREDIENTS

Serves 4–8

3 strips bacon, diced
1½ pounds assorted fresh fish, skinned, boned and diced
1 tablespoon paprika, plus extra to garnish
6¼ cups fish stock or water
3 firm tomatoes, peeled and chopped
4 waxy potatoes, peeled and grated
1–2 teaspoons chopped fresh marjoram, plus extra to garnish

For the dumplings
½ cup semolina or all-purpose flour
1 egg, beaten
3 tablespoons milk or water
generous pinch of salt
1 tablespoon chopped fresh parsley

1 Dry-fry the diced bacon in a large pan until pale golden brown, then add the pieces of assorted fish. Fry for 1–2 minutes, being careful not to break up the pieces of fish.

2 Sprinkle in the paprika, pour in the fish stock or water, bring to a boil and simmer for 10 minutes.

3 Stir the tomatoes, grated potato and marjoram into the pan. Cook for 10 minutes, stirring occasionally.

4 Meanwhile, make the dumplings by combining all the ingredients, then let stand, covered with plastic wrap, for 5–10 minutes.

5 Drop spoonfuls into the soup and cook for 10 minutes. Serve hot, with a little marjoram and paprika.

Hungarian Sour Cherry Soup

Particularly popular in summer, this fruit soup is typical of Hungarian cooking. The recipe makes good use of the plump, sour cherries available locally. Fruit soups are thickened with flour, and a touch of salt is added to help bring out the flavor of this cold soup.

INGREDIENTS

Serves 4

1 tablespoon all-purpose flour
$\frac{1}{2}$ cup sour cream
generous pinch of salt
1 teaspoon sugar
1$\frac{1}{2}$ cups fresh sour or morello
    cherries, pitted
3$\frac{3}{4}$ cups water
$\frac{1}{4}$ cup sugar

1 Blend the flour with the sour cream; add the salt and sugar.

2 Cook the cherries in the water, with the sugar. Gently poach for about 10 minutes.

— COOK'S TIP —

The soup is best made with fresh sour or cooking cherries such as morello; the flavor is simply not the same when canned or frozen cherries are used.

3 Remove from heat and set aside 2 tablespoons of the cooking liquid as a garnish. Stir another 2 tablespoons of the cherry liquid into the flour and sour cream mixture, then pour this on the cherries.

4 Return to the heat. Bring to a boil, then simmer for 5–6 minutes.

5 Remove from heat, cover with plastic wrap and let cool. Add extra salt if necessary. Serve with a little cooking liquid swirled in.

Czech Pork Soup

Originally, this soup would have been made from a half or quarter of a pig's head, but these days a shoulder of pork is a little easier to procure and just as tasty.

INGREDIENTS

Serves 4–6

12 ounces lean shoulder of pork or
    tenderloin, cut into $\frac{1}{2}$-inch cubes
1 large onion, finely sliced
$\frac{2}{3}$ cup carrots, finely diced
3 garlic cloves, crushed
6$\frac{1}{4}$ cups water or pork stock
2 teaspoons chopped fresh marjoram
4–6 tablespoons freshly cooked pearl
    barley or long-grain rice
salt and freshly ground black pepper

1 Put the pork cubes, onion, carrot and garlic in a large pan. Pour in the water or stock.

— COOK'S TIP —

For a more substantial soup, double the amount of barley or rice.

2 Simmer for 1–1$\frac{1}{2}$ hours or until the meat is just tender.

3 Skim, if necessary, before adding the marjoram. Season to taste. Simmer for another 5–10 minutes.

4 Place the barley or rice in serving bowls, then ladle on the soup.

Stuffed Mushrooms with Spinach

Large, flat, wild or cultivated mushrooms are excellent in this recipe, but use fresh cèpes instead for perfection.

INGREDIENTS

Serves 6

12 large flat mushrooms
1 pound small baby spinach leaves, well washed
3 strips bacon, cut into ¼-inch dice
1 onion, finely chopped
2 egg yolks, beaten
¾ cup fresh bread crumbs
1 teaspoon chopped fresh marjoram
3 tablespoons olive or vegetable oil
1 cup feta cheese, crumbled
salt and freshly ground black pepper

1 Peel the mushrooms only if necessary. Remove the stalks and chop them finely.

2 Blanch the spinach by dropping into a pan of boiling water for 1–2 minutes, then plunge into cold water. Squeeze the spinach in paper towels, drying it thoroughly to prevent the filling from being watery, then chop.

3 Dry-fry the diced bacon strips and chopped onion together in a pan until golden brown, then add the mushroom stalks. Remove from heat. Stir in the spinach, egg yolks, fresh bread crumbs and marjoram and season to taste.

4 Place the mushrooms on a baking sheet and brush with a little oil.

5 Place heaping tablespoons of the spinach mixture on the mushroom caps. Sprinkle on the cheese and cook the mushrooms under a preheated broiler for about 10 minutes or until golden brown.

Potato Pancakes

These little snacks are popular street food in the Czech Republic, and they are available at roadside stalls and cafés. Quick and easy to make, they are a tasty adaptation of the classic flour-based pancake.

INGREDIENTS

Serves 6–8
6 large waxy potatoes, peeled
2 eggs, beaten
1–2 garlic cloves, crushed
1 cup all-purpose flour
1 teaspoon chopped fresh marjoram
4 tablespoons butter
4 tablespoons oil
salt and freshly ground black pepper
sour cream, chopped fresh parsley and
   a tomato salad, to serve

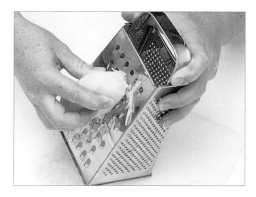

1 Grate the potatoes and squeeze thoroughly dry, using a dish towel.

3 Heat half the butter and oil together in a large frying pan, then add large spoonfuls of the potato mixture to form rounds. Carefully flatten the "pancakes" well with the back of a dampened spoon.

4 Fry the pancakes until crisp and golden brown, then turn over and cook on the other side. Drain on paper towels and keep warm while cooking the rest of the pancakes, adding the remaining butter and oil to the frying pan as necessary.

2 Put the potatoes in a bowl with the eggs, garlic, flour, marjoram and seasoning and mix well.

—————— COOK'S TIP ——————

Put the potatoes in water with a few drops of lemon, to prevent them from turning brown.

5 Serve the pancakes topped with sour cream, sprinkled with parsley, and accompanied by a fresh, juicy tomato salad.

Herbed Liver Pâté Pie

A delicious luncheon dish with a glass of Pilsen beer.

INGREDIENTS

Serves 10

1½ pounds ground pork
12 ounces pork liver
2 cups cooked ham, diced
1 small onion, finely chopped
2 tablespoons chopped fresh parsley
1 teaspoon German mustard
2 tablespoons Kirsch
1 teaspoon salt
beaten egg, for sealing and glazing
1 ounce envelope aspic jelly
1 cup boiling water
freshly ground black pepper
bread and dill pickles, to serve

For the pastry

4 cups all-purpose flour
pinch of salt
1¼ cups butter
2 eggs
1 egg yolk
2 tablespoons water

1 Preheat the oven to 400°F. To make the pastry, sift the flour and salt and rub in the butter. Beat the eggs, egg yolk and water, add to the dry ingredients and mix.

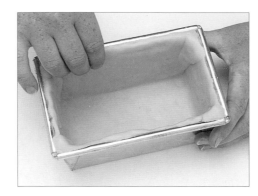

2 Knead the dough briefly until smooth. Roll out two-thirds on a lightly floured surface and use to line a 4 × 10-inch hinged loaf pan. Trim any excess dough.

3 Process half the pork and the liver until fairly smooth. Stir in the remaining ground pork, ham, onion, parsley, mustard, Kirsch and seasoning.

4 Spoon the filling into the pan, smoothing it down and leveling the surface.

5 Roll out the remaining pastry on the lightly floured surface and use it to top the pie, sealing the edges with some of the beaten egg. Decorate with the pastry trimmings and glaze with the remaining beaten egg. Using a fork, make 3 or 4 holes in the top, for the steam to escape.

6 Bake for 40 minutes, then reduce the oven temperature to 350°F and cook for another hour. Cover the pastry with aluminum foil if the top begins to brown too much. Let the pie cool in the pan.

7 Make the aspic jelly, using the boiling water. Stir to dissolve, then let cool.

8 Make a small hole near the edge of the pie with a skewer, then pour in the aspic through a waxed paper funnel. Chill for at least 2 hours before serving the pie in slices with mustard, bread and dill pickles.

Vegetable Salad

This salad is a delicious blend of typical Central East European ingredients—sour cream, dill pickle, lemon juice and paprika. It is generally served as an appetizer alongside cold meats or poultry.

INGREDIENTS

Serves 6

1½ cups green beans, trimmed
2 carrots, diced
1 cup fresh or frozen peas
6 egg yolks
1 tablespoon German mustard
2 tablespoons sugar
3 tablespoons freshly squeezed
    lemon juice
1⅔ cups sour cream
1 small apple, cored and diced
2–3 celery stalks, diced
1 dill pickle, diced
3 hard-boiled eggs
1 teaspoon chopped fresh parsley
2 tablespoons fresh bread crumbs
1 teaspoon paprika
salt and freshly ground black pepper

1 Cook the green beans, carrots and peas in a large saucepan of boiling salted water for 5–8 minutes. Drain well, then plunge into cold water to refresh. Drain well again.

2 Blend together in a heatproof bowl the egg yolks, mustard, sugar, lemon juice, sour cream and seasoning. Place the bowl containing the mixture over a pan of simmering water, stirring constantly, until the sauce starts to thicken.

3 Remove from heat and stir in the cooked vegetables, apple, celery and dill pickle. Mix well, then cover and chill.

4 Cut the hard-boiled eggs in half lengthwise and carefully remove the yolks into a small mixing bowl, keeping the egg whites intact.

5 Blend the cooked egg yolks well with the parsley, bread crumbs, paprika and a little seasoning. Use the filling to stuff the egg whites. Arrange the chilled vegetables on a serving plate and top with the stuffed eggs.

COOK'S TIP

If German mustard is too strong, replace with either a grainy mustard or chopped fresh tarragon.

MEAT AND POULTRY

*Lamb, beef, veal and chicken are all used in Central European cook
though it is perhaps pork that best exemplifies German and Centr
European meat cooking. Roasts feature often, as do casseroles and stews
are often served with dumplings. The sweet-sour flavor so typical acros
region is again in evidence with sauces and meat stews containing dill p
and sauerkraut. In Hungary, however, the presence of paprika, introduce
Turkey, has led to many classic dishes, of which Goulash is just on*

Leg of Lamb with Pickle Sauce

Lamb is generally reserved for special occasions and festivals in Hungary. The sourness of the pickle sauce is an unusual contrast to the rich lamb.

INGREDIENTS

Serves 6–8
4 pounds lean leg of lamb
2–3 tablespoons sea salt
finely grated zest of 1 lemon
$^{1}/_{4}$ cup butter
4 rosemary sprigs
handful of flat-leaf parsley
extra sprigs of rosemary and flat-leaf
    parsley, to garnish
braised red cabbage,
    to serve

For the pickle sauce
8–10 gherkins
2 tablespoons butter
$^{1}/_{2}$ cup all-purpose flour
1 cup lamb stock
generous pinch of saffron threads
2 tablespoons sour cream
1–2 teaspoons white wine vinegar
salt and freshly ground black pepper

1 Preheat the oven to 350°F. Flatten the lamb with a rolling pin, rub with salt; set aside for 30 minutes.

2 Combine the lemon zest and butter. Place the lamb in a roasting pan and spread on the lemon butter.

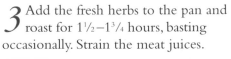

3 Add the fresh herbs to the pan and roast for $1^{1}/_{2}$–$1^{3}/_{4}$ hours, basting occasionally. Strain the meat juices.

4 Meanwhile, make the pickle sauce. Process the gherkins coarsely. Heat the butter in a small pan and cook the gherkins for 5 minutes, stirring occasionally. Remove from heat. Sprinkle in the flour and stir for another 2–3 minutes.

5 Slowly pour the stock into the pan and bring to a boil. Stir in the saffron. Let the sauce simmer for another 15 minutes.

6 Off the heat, stir in the sour cream, vinegar and the strained meat juices. Season to taste. Garnish with herbs and serve with the sauce and red cabbage.

COOK'S TIP

Let the lamb stand for 10–20 minutes after cooking to let the fibers in the meat relax, making it more tender, firmer and easier to carve.

Lamb Goulash with Tomatoes and Bell Peppers

Goulash is a dish that has traveled across Europe from Hungary and is popular in many places, such as the Czech Republic and Germany. This Czech recipe is not a true goulash, however, because of the addition of flour. Nevertheless, it has a wonderful infusion of tomatoes, paprika, green bell peppers and marjoram.

INGREDIENTS

Serves 4–6

2 tablespoons vegetable oil or melted lard (optional)
2 pounds lean lamb, trimmed and cut into cubes
1 large onion, roughly chopped
2 garlic cloves, crushed
3 green bell peppers, seeded and diced
2 tablespoons paprika
2 14-ounce cans chopped plum tomatoes
1 tablespoon chopped fresh flat-leaf parsley
1 teaspoon chopped fresh marjoram
2 tablespoons all-purpose flour
$^1\!/_4$ cup cold water
salt and freshly ground black pepper
green salad, to serve

1 Heat up the oil or lard, if using, in a frying pan. Dry-fry or fry the pieces of lamb for 5–8 minutes or until browned on all sides. Season well.

2 Add the onion and garlic and cook for another 2 minutes before adding the green peppers and paprika.

3 Pour in the tomatoes and enough water, if needed, to cover the meat in the pan. Stir in the herbs. Bring to a boil, turn down the heat, cover and simmer very gently for $1^1\!/_2$ hours or until the lamb is tender.

4 Blend the flour with the cold water and pour into the stew. Bring back to a boil, then reduce the heat to a simmer and cook until the sauce has thickened. Adjust the seasoning and serve the lamb goulash with a crisp green salad.

Loin of Pork with Prune Stuffing

Pork is by far the most popular meat in Germany and appears in many guises. Crushed gingersnaps are a traditional thickening ingredient and add color and flavor to the sauce.

INGREDIENTS

Serves 4

3 pounds cured or smoked loin
   of pork
about 18 prunes, finely chopped
3 tablespoons apple juice or water
1½ cups day-old gingersnap crumbs
3 cardamom pods
1 tablespoon sunflower oil
1 onion, chopped
1 cup dry red wine
1 tablespoon dark brown sugar
salt and freshly ground black pepper
buttery fried pitted prunes and apple
   and leek slices with steamed green
   cabbage, to serve

1 Preheat the oven to 450°F. Put the pork, fat-side down, on a board. Make a cut about 1¼ inches deep along the length to within ½ inch of the ends, then make 2 deep cuts to its left and right, to create 2 pockets in the meat.

2 Put the prunes in a bowl. Spoon on the apple juice or water, then add the cookie crumbs. Remove the cardamom seeds from their pods and crush using a mortar and pestle, or on a board with the end of a rolling pin. Add to the bowl with salt and pepper.

3 Mix the prune stuffing well and use to fill the pockets in the meat.

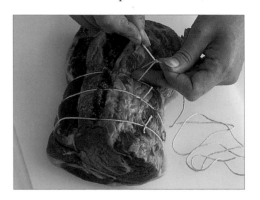

4 Tie the pork at regular intervals with string. Heat the oil in a roasting pan set on the stove and brown the pork over high heat. Remove the meat and set aside.

5 Add the chopped onion to the pan and sauté for 10 minutes, until golden. Return the pork to the pan, pour in the wine and add the sugar and seasoning.

6 Roast for 10 minutes, then reduce the oven temperature to 350°F and roast, uncovered, for another hour and 50 minutes or until cooked and golden brown.

7 Remove the pork from the pan and keep warm. Strain the meat juices through a sieve into a pan and simmer for 10 minutes, until slightly reduced. Carve the pork and serve with the sauce separately, accompanied by buttery fried prunes and apple and leek slices, together with steamed green cabbage.

Braised Spicy Spareribs

Choose really meaty ribs for this dish and trim off any excess fat before cooking, as the juices are turned into a delicious sauce.

INGREDIENTS

Serves 6

¹/₄ cup all-purpose flour
1 teaspoon salt
1 teaspoon ground black pepper
3¹/₂ pounds pork spareribs, cut into
   individual pieces
2 tablespoons sunflower oil
1 onion, finely chopped
1 garlic clove, crushed
3 tablespoons tomato paste
2 tablespoons chili sauce
2 tablespoons red wine vinegar
pinch of ground cloves
2¹/₂ cups beef stock
1 tablespoon cornstarch
flat-leaf parsley, to garnish
sauerkraut and crusty bread, to serve

1 Preheat the oven to 350°F. Combine the flour, salt and black pepper in a shallow dish. Add the ribs and toss to coat them in flour.

2 Heat the oil in a large frying pan and cook the ribs, turning them until well browned. Transfer them to a roasting pan and sprinkle on the chopped onion.

3 In a bowl, combine the garlic, tomato paste, chili sauce, vinegar, cloves and stock. Pour over the ribs, then cover with aluminum foil. Roast for 1¹/₂ hours or until tender, removing the foil for the last 30 minutes.

4 Transfer the juices from the roasting pan to a small pan. Blend the cornstarch in a cup with a little cold water and stir in. Bring the sauce to a boil, stirring, then simmer for 2–3 minutes, until thickened.

5 Arrange the ribs on a bed of sauerkraut, then pour on a little sauce. Serve the remaining sauce separately in a warmed bowl. Garnish with flat-leaf parsley and serve with sauerkraut and crusty bread.

COOK'S TIP

If time allows, first marinate the ribs in sunflower oil mixed with red wine vinegar

Pork Stew with Sauerkraut

An excellent combination of classic Central European flavors.

INGREDIENTS

Serves 4–6
2 tablespoons vegetable oil or lard
2 onions, finely chopped
2 garlic cloves, crushed
2 pounds lean pork, cut into
    2-inch cubes
1 teaspoon caraway seeds (optional)
1 tablespoon chopped fresh dill
3¾ cups warm pork or
    vegetable stock
4 cups sauerkraut, drained
1 tablespoon paprika
salt
dill, to garnish
sour cream, sprinkled with paprika,
    and pickled chiles (optional),
    to serve

1 Heat the oil or lard in a large pan and cook the onion and crushed garlic cloves until soft.

2 Add the pork cubes to the pan and fry until browned. Stir in the caraway seeds, if using, and fresh dill, and pour in the stock. Cook for 1 hour over low heat.

3 Stir the drained sauerkraut into the pork with the paprika. Let simmer gently for 45 minutes. Add salt, to taste.

4 Garnish the stew with a little more dill and serve with sour cream sprinkled with paprika, with pickled chiles, if desired.

Pork and Garlic Sausage Casserole

This hearty and filling casserole contains a variety of pork cuts. The light ale helps tenderize and flavor the meat.

INGREDIENTS

Serves 6
3 tablespoons sunflower oil
8 ounces bacon, diced
1 pound lean shoulder of pork,
    trimmed and cut into 1-inch cubes
1 large onion, sliced
2 pounds potatoes, thickly sliced
1 cup light ale
2 cups German garlic sausage,
    skinned and sliced
2¼ cups sauerkraut, drained
2 red apples, cored and sliced
1 teaspoon caraway seeds
salt and freshly ground black pepper

1 Preheat the oven to 350°F. Heat 2 tablespoons of the oil in a flameproof casserole. Fry the bacon for 2–3 minutes, then lightly brown the cubes of pork. Set aside.

2 Add the remaining oil to the pan and gently cook the onion for 10 minutes, until soft. Return the meat to the pan and add the potatoes.

4 Stir in the garlic sausage, drained sauerkraut, sliced apple and caraway seeds. Season with salt and pepper. Return to the oven and cook the casserole for another 30 minutes or until the meat is tender.

3 Stir in the ale and bring to a boil. Cover and cook for 45 minutes.

Veal Roast

Veal is often flattened, then layered or rolled around fillings. This mixture of veal, bacon, egg and ham as a filling is delicious.

INGREDIENTS

Serves 4–6

3 pounds shoulder of veal or lean pork, cut into ³/₄-inch slices
8 ounces bacon
6 ounces sliced ham
4 eggs, beaten
3 tablespoons milk
3 dill pickles, finely diced
¹/₂ cup butter
3 tablespoons all-purpose flour
1¹/₂ cups water or chicken stock
salt and freshly ground black pepper
baby carrots, green beans and dill pickle slices, to serve

1 Preheat the oven to 350°F. Place the veal or pork between 2 pieces of plastic wrap and pound or flatten into a regular shape using a meat mallet or rolling pin. Season well.

2 Top each slice of veal or pork with a layer of bacon and ham. Beat the eggs in a small pan with the milk and stir over low heat until the mixture is softly scrambled. Let cool a little.

3 Place a layer of the scrambled eggs on top of each slice and spread with a knife, then sprinkle on the finely diced dill pickle.

4 Carefully roll up each slice. Tie the rolls securely at regular intervals with string.

5 Heat the butter in a large flameproof casserole. Add the meat rolls and brown on all sides. Remove the pan from heat. Remove the rolls and set aside. Sprinkle the flour into the pan and stir well.

6 Return the pan to the heat and cook the flour mixture until pale brown, then slowly add half of the water. Return the meat rolls to the pan and bring to a boil, then put the casserole in the oven for 1³/₄–2 hours to roast slowly, adding the remaining water during cooking if necessary to prevent the veal from drying out.

7 When cooked, let the rolls stand for 10 minutes, before serving in slices with the gravy and baby carrots, green beans and dill pickles.

Hungarian Goulash

Paprika is a distinctive feature of Hungarian cooking. It is a spicy seasoning ground from a variety of sweet red pepper, which has been grown in Hungary since the end of the 16th century. Shepherds added the spice to their *gulyás*, and fishermen used it in their stews.

INGREDIENTS

Serves 4–6
2 tablespoons vegetable oil or
   melted lard
2 onions, chopped
2 pounds braising or stewing beef,
   trimmed and cubed
1 garlic clove, crushed
generous pinch of caraway seeds
2 tablespoons paprika
1 firm ripe tomato, chopped
10 cups beef stock
2 green bell peppers, seeded and sliced
1 pound potatoes, diced
salt

For the dumplings
2 eggs, beaten
6 tablespoons all-purpose flour, sifted

1 Heat the oil or lard in a large heavy pan. Add the onion and cook until soft.

2 Add the beef cubes to the pan and cook for 10 minutes, browning gently, stirring frequently to prevent the meat from sticking.

3 Add the garlic, caraway seeds and a little salt to the pan. Remove from heat and stir in the paprika and tomato. Pour in the beef stock and cook, covered, over low heat for 1–1½ hours or until tender.

4 Add the peppers and potatoes to the pan and cook for another 20–25 minutes, stirring occasionally.

5 Meanwhile, make the dumplings by combining the beaten eggs with the flour and a little salt. With lightly floured hands, roll out the dumplings and drop them into the simmering stew for 2–3 minutes or until they rise to the surface of the stew. Adjust the seasoning and serve the goulash in warm dishes.

Sauerbraten

A classic sweet-sour marinade gives this dish its name.

INGREDIENTS

Serves 6

2¼ pounds silverside of beef
2 tablespoons sunflower oil
1 onion, sliced
4 ounces bacon, diced
1 tablespoon cornstarch
1 cup crushed gingersnaps
flat-leaf parsley, to garnish
buttered noodles, to serve

For the marinade

2 onions, sliced
1 carrot, sliced
2 celery stalks, sliced
2½ cups water
⅔ cup red vinegar
1 bay leaf
6 cloves
6 whole black peppercorns
1 tablespoon dark brown sugar
2 teaspoons salt

1 To make the marinade, put the onions, carrot and celery in a pan with the water. Bring to a boil and simmer for 5 minutes. Add the remaining marinade ingredients and simmer for another 5 minutes. Cover and let cool.

2 Put the beef in a casserole into which it just fits. Pour on the marinade, cover and let marinate in the refrigerator for 3 days if possible, turning daily.

3 Remove the beef from the marinade and dry thoroughly using paper towels. Heat the oil in a large frying pan and brown the beef over high heat. Remove the beef and set aside. Add the sliced onion to the pan and sauté for 5 minutes. Add the bacon and cook for another 5 minutes or until lightly browned.

4 Strain the marinade, reserving the liquid. Put the onion and bacon in a large flameproof casserole or pan, then put the beef on top. Pour on the marinade liquid. Slowly bring to a boil, cover, then simmer over low heat for 1½–2 hours or until the beef is very tender.

5 Remove the beef and keep warm. Blend the cornstarch in a cup with a little cold water. Add to the cooking liquid with the gingersnap crumbs and bring to a boil, stirring. Thickly slice the beef and serve on a bed of hot buttered noodles. Garnish with sprigs of fresh flat-leaf parsley and pass the gravy separately.

Chicken with Wild Mushrooms and Garlic

This roasted chicken dish has a hint of fresh herbs.

INGREDIENTS

Serves 4

3 tablespoons olive or vegetable oil
3-pound chicken
1 large onion, finely chopped
3 celery stalks, chopped
2 garlic cloves, crushed
4 cups fresh wild mushrooms,
  sliced if large
1 teaspoon chopped fresh thyme
1 cup chicken stock
1 cup dry white wine
juice of 1 lemon
2 tablespoons chopped fresh parsley
½ cup sour cream
salt and freshly ground black pepper
flat-leaf parsley, to garnish
fresh green beans, to serve

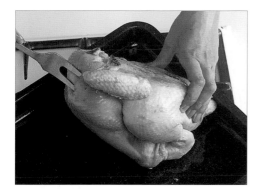

1 Preheat the oven to 375°F. Heat the oil in a roasting pan and brown the chicken all over.

2 Add the onion and cook for about 2 minutes. Add the next 4 ingredients and cook for 3 minutes.

3 Pour the chicken stock, wine and lemon juice into the roasting pan. Sprinkle on half of the parsley and season well. Place the chicken in the oven and cook for 1½–1¾ hours or until tender, basting occasionally to prevent it from drying out.

> — COOK'S TIP —
>
> Clean wild mushrooms well to remove any dirt, or use cultured mushrooms instead.

4 Remove the chicken from the roasting pan and keep warm. Put the roasting pan on the stove and stir in the sour cream over low heat, adding a little extra stock or water if necessary to make the juices into a thick pouring sauce.

5 Arrange the chicken on a plate, surrounded by the creamy mushrooms. Garnish with the parsley sprigs and serve the chicken with the sauce and fresh green beans.

Chicken in Badacsonyi Wine

In Hungary, this recipe is made with a Balatan wine called *Badacsonyi Këkryalii* ("Blue Handled"), which has a full body and distinctive bouquet.

INGREDIENTS

Serves 4

¹/₄ cup butter
4 scallions, chopped
4 ounces bacon, diced
2 bay leaves
1 tarragon sprig
3-pound chicken
¹/₄ cup sweet sherry or mead
scant 2 cups button mushrooms, sliced
1¹/₄ cups *Badacsonyi* or dry white wine
salt
tarragon and bay leaves,
   to garnish
fresh steamed rice, to serve

1 Heat the butter in a large heavy pan or flameproof casserole and sweat the scallions for 1–1¹/₂ minutes. Add the bacon, bay leaves and the tarragon, stripping the leaves from the stem. Cook for another 1 minute.

--- COOK'S TIP ---

Traditionally, this recipe also used a sweet drink with a honeyed caramel flavor called márc. If this is not available, replace it with sweet sherry or mead.

2 Add the whole chicken to the pan and pour in the sweet sherry or mead. Cook, covered, over very low heat for 15 minutes.

3 Sprinkle the mushrooms into the pan and pour in the wine. Cook, covered, for another 1 hour. Remove the lid, baste the chicken with the wine mixture and cook, uncovered, for another 30 minutes, until almost all the liquid has evaporated.

4 Skim the cooking liquid remaining in the pan. Season to taste and remove the chicken, vegetables and bacon to a serving dish. Garnish with tarragon and bay leaves and serve with freshly cooked rice.

Roast Goose with Apples

Ganzebraten mit Apfeln symbolizes Christmas dinner in Germany. Here it is served with hazelnut- and honey-stuffed apples.

INGREDIENTS

Serves 6

scant 1 cup raisins
finely grated zest and juice of 1 orange
2 tablespoons butter
1 onion, finely chopped
³/₄ cup hazelnuts, chopped
3 cups fresh white bread crumbs
1 tablespoon honey
1 tablespoon chopped fresh marjoram
2 tablespoons chopped fresh parsley
6 apples
1 tablespoon lemon juice
10–11-pound oven-ready
  young goose
salt and freshly ground black pepper
fresh herbs, to garnish
orange wedges, red cabbage and green
  beans, to serve

1 Preheat the oven to 425°F. Put the raisins in a bowl and pour in the orange juice. Melt the butter in a frying pan and then gently cook the onion for 5 minutes.

2 Add the chopped nuts to the pan and cook for another 4–5 minutes or until beginning to brown.

3 Add the cooked onion and nuts to the raisins with 1 cup of the bread crumbs, the orange zest, honey, herbs and seasoning. Mix well.

4 Wash the apples and remove the cores to leave a ³/₄-inch hole. Using a sharp knife, make a shallow cut around the middle of each apple. Brush the cut and the cavity with the lemon juice to prevent it from browning.

5 Pack the center of each apple with the nut and raisin stuffing.

6 Mix the remaining bread crumbs into the stuffing and stuff the bird's tail end. Close with a small skewer.

7 Place the goose in a roasting pan, then prick the skin all over with a skewer. Roast for 30 minutes, then reduce the oven temperature to 350°F and cook for another 3 hours, pouring the excess fat out of the pan several times.

8 Arrange the apples around the goose and bake for 30–40 minutes or until tender. Rest the goose in a warm place for 15 minutes, before carving. Garnish with fresh herbs, stuffed apples and orange wedges, with red cabbage and green beans.

COOK'S TIP

To test whether the goose is cooked, pierce the thigh with a thin skewer. The juice that runs out should be pale yellow. If it is tinged with pink, roast the goose for another 10 minutes and test again.

FISH

Indigenous central European freshwater fish include carp, pike, trout, bream and wels, a type of catfish. A popular saltwater fish is cod. Fresh fish is often baked or poached and served with sauces, such as the German recipe for Cod in Mustard Sauce or the Czech recipe for Carp in Black Sauce. Many of these recipes have remained unchanged for generations—such as Hungarian Fish Sausages dating from the 17th century and German Blue Trout— and are still the best way to appreciate the distinctive flavors of these fish.

Baked Pike with Wild Mushrooms

Pike is a large family of fish found in the rivers of Europe. It has a good, fresh flavor and firm white flesh, making it perfect for baking in a creamy-paprika sauce with wild mushrooms and bell peppers.

INGREDIENTS

Serves 4–6

3-pound whole pike or perch
½ cup butter
½ cup finely sliced onion
3 cups wild mushrooms,
 roughly sliced
1 tablespoon paprika
1½ tablespoons all-purpose flour
1 cup sour cream
1 tablespoon finely chopped
 green bell pepper
salt and freshly ground black pepper

1 Preheat the oven to 375°F. Clean, skin and fillet the fish and put the bones and skin in a large pan. Cover with cold water and bring to a boil. Reduce the heat, season and simmer for 30 minutes.

COOK'S TIP

Perch or any firm-fleshed white fish can be used instead of pike.

2 Meanwhile, butter a roasting pan, add the fillets and lightly season.

3 Melt the remaining butter in a pan and add the onion. Cook gently for 3–4 minutes, before adding the mushrooms. Cook for another 2–3 minutes then sprinkle in the paprika.

4 Strain the fish stock, ladle out 1 cup and pour into the onion and mushrooms.

5 Blend the flour with the sour cream, stir into the pan, then pour over the fish. Bake for 30 minutes or until just tender. Sprinkle the green pepper over the top of the onion and mushroom mixture just before serving.

Carp in Black Sauce

This Czech dish is usually served on Christmas Eve. The carp is generally sold alive and then kept in fresh clean water—often in the bathtub—until needed.

INGREDIENTS

Serves 4

4 tablespoons butter
1 onion, sliced
2 carrots, diced
2 small parsnips, diced
¼ small celeriac, diced
juice of 1 lemon
¼ cup red wine vinegar
¾ cup dark ale
8 whole black peppercorns
½ teaspoon allspice
1 bay leaf
1 teaspoon chopped fresh thyme
¾-inch piece ginger root,
   peeled and grated
1 strip of lemon peel
3 slices of dark pumpernickel bread,
   processed into crumbs
2 tablespoons all-purpose flour
1 tablespoon sugar
⅓ cup raisins
6 prunes
2 tablespoons hazelnuts and almonds,
   roughly chopped
4 thick carp or sea bream steaks
salt and freshly ground black pepper
fresh snipped chives, to garnish
dumplings and fresh bread, to serve

1 Melt half of the butter in a flame-proof casserole. Add the onion and cook for 2–3 minutes, then stir in the carrots, parsnips and celeriac. Cook for another 5 minutes.

2 Stir in the lemon juice, red wine vinegar and dark ale. Pour in just enough water to cover.

3 Place the peppercorns, allspice, bay leaf, thyme, ginger, lemon peel and a little seasoning, in a bowl. Stir in the bread crumbs, mix well and add to the vegetables. Simmer for 15 minutes.

4 Meanwhile, melt the remaining butter in a small pan and sprinkle in the flour. Cook gently for 1–2 minutes before adding the sugar. Cook for another 2–3 minutes or until the sugar caramelizes.

5 Gradually ladle all of the stock from the casserole into the flour mixture; stir well, then pour this back into the vegetable mixture. Add the raisins, prunes and nuts, and seasoning.

6 Place the fish steaks on top of the vegetables and cook for 12–15 minutes. To serve, arrange the fish on dishes, strain the vegetables, nuts and fruit and place them around the fish. Reduce the sauce by boiling quickly. Garnish with snipped chives and serve with dumplings and fresh bread.

Fish Goulash

This wholesome meal is a cross between a stew and a soup. It is traditionally served with a hot cherry pepper in the center of the serving plate and the goulash ladled over it.

INGREDIENTS

Serves 6

4¹/₂ pounds mixed fish
4 large onions, sliced
2 garlic cloves, crushed
¹/₂ small celeriac, diced
handful of parsley stalks or
    cleaned roots
2 tablespoons paprika
1 green bell pepper, seeded and sliced
1–2 teaspoons tomato paste
salt
6 tablespoons sour cream and
    3 cherry peppers (optional),
    to serve

1 Skin and fillet the fish and cut the flesh into chunks. Put all the fish heads, skin and bones into a large pan, together with the onions, garlic, celeriac, parsley stalks, paprika and salt. Cover with water and bring to a boil. Reduce the heat and simmer for 1¹/₄ –1¹/₂ hours. Strain the stock.

2 Place the fish and green pepper in a large frying pan and pour in the stock. Blend the tomato paste with a little stock and pour it into the pan.

3 Heat gently, but do not stir, or the fish will break up. Cook for just 10–12 minutes but do not boil. Season to taste. Ladle into warmed deep plates or bowls and top with a generous spoonful of sour cream and a halved cherry pepper, if desired.

Fish Sausages

This recipe has featured in many Hungarian cookbooks since the 17th century.

INGREDIENTS

Serves 3–4

13 ounces fish fillets, such as perch,
    pike, carp, cod, skinned
1 white bread roll
5 tablespoons milk
1¹/₂ tablespoons chopped fresh
    flat-leaf parsley
2 eggs, well beaten
¹/₂ cup all-purpose flour
1 cup fine fresh white bread crumbs
oil, for shallow-frying
salt and freshly ground black pepper
deep-fried sprigs of parsley and lemon
    wedges, sprinkled with paprika,
    to serve

1 Grind or process the fish coarsely in a food processor or blender. Soak the roll in the milk for about 10 minutes, then squeeze it out. Combine the fish and bread before adding the chopped parsley, one of the eggs and seasoning.

2 Using your fingers, shape the mixture into 4-inch long sausages, about 1 inch thick.

3 Carefully roll the fish "sausages" into the flour, then in the remaining egg and then lastly in the bread crumbs.

4 Heat the oil in a pan, then slowly cook the "sausages" until golden brown all over. Drain well on crumpled paper towels. Garnish with deep-fried parsley sprigs and lemon wedges sprinkled with paprika.

Blue Trout

The blue sheen of *Blaue Forelle* is a German specialty and is easily achieved by first scalding the fish and then fanning to cool it. Traditionally the fish was left to cool in a breeze or draft.

INGREDIENTS

Serves 4
4 trout, about 6 ounces each
1 teaspoon salt
2½ cups white wine vinegar
1 onion, sliced
2 bay leaves
6 whole black peppercorns
bay leaves and lemon slices, to garnish
½ cup melted butter
creamed horseradish sauce and
   green beans, to serve

1 Preheat the oven to 350°F. Rub both sides of the trout with salt and place in a non-aluminum roasting pan or fish kettle.

2 Bring the vinegar to a boil and slowly pour over the trout. Fan the fish as it cools or let stand in a draft for 5 minutes.

3 Bring the vinegar back to a boil, then add the sliced onion, bay leaves and peppercorns.

4 Cover the pan with aluminum foil and cook for 30 minutes or until the fish is cooked. Transfer the fish to warmed serving dishes, garnish with bay leaves and lemon slices, and serve with melted butter, creamed horseradish sauce and green beans.

Baked Salmon

This Czech recipe uses freshwater fish such as salmon or trout but saltwater fish such as mackerel can also be used. It is a very simple but tasty meal, as the fish cooks in its own juices.

INGREDIENTS

Serves 6
4-pound whole salmon
½ cup butter, melted
½–1 teaspoon caraway seeds
3 tablespoons lemon juice
salt and freshly ground pepper
sprigs of flat-leaf parsley and lemon
   wedges, to garnish

COOK'S TIP

Take care when cutting the fish: dip your fingers into a little salt to help you grip the fish better.

---

1 Preheat the oven to 350°F. Using a sharp knife, cut the fish in half lengthwise.

2 Place the salmon, skin-side down, in a lightly greased roasting pan and brush with the melted butter. Season, and sprinkle on the caraway seeds and then the lemon juice.

3 Bake the salmon, loosely covered with aluminum foil, for 25 minutes or until the flesh flakes easily.

4 Transfer the fish to a serving plate. Garnish with flat-leaf parsley and lemon wedges. Serve hot or cold.

Marinated Fish

With a number of tart flavors, this is a strong, zesty marinade.

INGREDIENTS

Serves 6–8
4 pounds tuna, carp or pike steaks
6 tablespoons butter, melted
¼ cup dry sherry
salt and freshly ground black pepper

For the marinade
1⅔ cups water
⅔ cup wine vinegar
⅔ cup good fish stock
1 onion, thinly sliced
6 white peppercorns
½ teaspoon allspice
2 cloves
1 bay leaf
1½ tablespoons bottled capers, drained and chopped
2 dill pickles, diced
½ cup olive oil
salad, dill pickles and bread, to serve

1 Preheat the oven to 350°F. Put the fish steaks into an ovenproof dish and brush with the butter. Sprinkle on the sherry. Season well and bake for 20–25 minutes or until just tender. Let cool.

COOK'S TIP

Use plump fillets of fish if tuna steaks are not available.

2 Meanwhile, boil the water, vinegar, fish stock, onion, spices and bay leaf together in a pan for 20 minutes. Let cool before adding the capers, dill pickle and olive oil.

3 Once the fish steaks have cooled, pour on the marinade.

4 Cover the dish with plastic wrap and marinate the fish for 24 hours in the refrigerator, basting occasionally. Serve with a green salad, dill pickles and slices of pumpernickel or rye bread.

Cod in Mustard Sauce

A firm, white-fleshed fish, cod is abundant in the North Sea and features in many German recipes. Reduced stock sauces, as in this dish, are replacing the heavier flour-based versions of former times.

INGREDIENTS

Serves 4

2 pounds cod fillets
1 lemon
1 small onion, sliced
¼ cup chopped fresh flat-leaf parsley, whole stalks reserved
6 allspice berries
6 whole black peppercorns
1 clove
1 bay leaf
5 cups water
2 tablespoons whole-grain mustard
6 tablespoons butter
salt and freshly ground black pepper
bay leaves, to garnish
boiled potatoes and carrots, to serve

1 Place the fish on a plate. Pare two thin strips of zest from the lemon, then squeeze the lemon for its juice. Sprinkle the juice on the fish.

2 Put the lemon zest in a large frying pan with the onion, the stalks from the parsley, the allspice, peppercorns, clove and bay leaf.

3 Pour in the water. Slowly bring to a boil, cover and simmer for 20 minutes. Add the fish, cover and cook *very* gently for 10 minutes.

4 Ladle 1 cup of the cooking liquid into a pan and simmer until reduced by half. Stir in the mustard.

5 Whisk the butter, a little at a time, into the reduced stock. Taste and season with salt and pepper, if needed.

6 Remove the fish from the stock and place on warmed serving dishes. Pour on a little sauce and serve the rest separately in a bowl. Garnish with chopped parsley and bay leaves and serve with boiled potatoes and carrots.

VEGETABLES, GRAINS AND PASTA

Home-grown vegetables form part of the local economy in much of rural central Europe. Vegetables may be pickled to preserve them throughout the year or used fresh in many interesting ways. Potatoes form an important part of the diet—served hot, made into potato cakes or eaten cold in salads. More popular in southern Germany is a pasta dish called Spätzle. Dried beans and pulses can be served on their own or as part of a main course to extend the protein in dishes, particularly in Czech and Hungarian cooking.

Kohlrabi Baked with Ham

Kohlrabi, which is German for "cabbage-turnip," is a member of the cabbage family with a delicate turnip-like taste. Kohlrabi may be purple or greenish-white and is delicious either raw, grated and sprinkled with salt, or cooked. The leaves can also be eaten—treat in the same way as spinach.

INGREDIENTS

Serves 4
½ cup butter
4 kohlrabi, peeled and diced
8 ounces thick ham, diced
2 tablespoons chopped fresh parsley

For the sauce
3 egg yolks
1 cup heavy cream
2 tablespoons all-purpose flour
pinch of mace
salt and freshly ground black pepper

1 Preheat the oven to 350°F. Melt the butter in a large frying pan and gently cook the kohlrabi for 8–10 minutes.

2 Arrange half of the kohlrabi in the bottom of a greased ovenproof dish. Top with the ham and parsley, and finish with the remaining kohlrabi.

> ——— COOK'S TIP ———
>
> Choose the smallest kohlrabi you can find, as these will have the freshest flavor.

3 Beat the sauce ingredients together and pour over the kohlrabi and ham. Bake for 30–35 minutes or until golden brown, and serve hot.

Poached Celery

This simple but tasty way of presenting celery is one that can also be used for kohlrabi, cauliflower or leeks. Select a hard cheese with medium to strong flavor.

INGREDIENTS

Serves 4
4 celery hearts
2 tablespoons butter
1 cup dry white wine
salt and freshly ground black pepper
1 tablespoon chopped fresh parsley,
  to garnish
grated cheese, to serve

1 Scrub the celery well and trim the ends. Cut the celery hearts in half lengthwise.

2 Parboil or blanch the celery in a pan of boiling salted water for 5 minutes. Drain and rinse quickly under cold water. Gently pat dry with paper towels.

3 Melt the butter in a frying pan and gently cook the celery for 1–2 minutes. Pour in the wine and bring to a boil. Reduce the heat to a simmer.

4 Cook uncovered for 5 minutes or until just tender. Drain well. Sprinkle with parsley and black pepper and serve with grated cheese on top.

Somogy Beans

This recipe comes from Somogy in Hungary, but every region has its own specialty. Serve with roast chicken, if desired.

INGREDIENTS

Serves 6–8

2½ cups dried white beans, such as haricots or white kidney beans, soaked overnight
1 bay leaf
8-ounce piece of bacon
1 tablespoon lard
1 onion, very finely chopped
2 garlic cloves, crushed
1 tablespoon all-purpose flour
1–2 tablespoons vinegar
generous pinch of sugar
½ cup sour cream
salt
sage leaves and paprika, to garnish

1 Drain the white beans (already soaked) and rinse well.

2 Put the beans in a large pan with the bay leaf, bacon and water to cover. Cook for 1¼–1½ hours or until the beans are tender. Carefully remove the bacon and dice when cool. Drain the beans, reserving ½ cup of the cooking liquid. (It may be useful to reserve a little more than this, in case it is needed in Step 5.)

3 Melt the lard in a frying pan and stir in the onion, garlic and flour. Cook for 2–3 minutes, then slowly stir in the reserved cooking liquid. Stir well.

4 Return the beans to a pan. Add the bacon and onion and stir well.

5 Add the vinegar, sugar and sour cream to the pan. Season to taste. If required, add a little more cooking liquid if the bean mixture is too stiff. Garnish with sage leaves and paprika.

COOK'S TIP

Salt is added only at the end of this recipe, otherwise the beans become tough.

Lecsó

Like much of Eastern Europe, Hungary makes good use of its fresh produce. Many of its vegetable recipes are substantial, flavorful dishes, intended to be eaten by themselves, as with this recipe, and not just as an accompaniment to meat, poultry or fish dishes.

Lecsó, in its most basic form of a thick tomato and onion purée, is also used as the basis for stews and other dishes.

INGREDIENTS

Serves 6–8
5 green bell peppers
2 tablespoons vegetable oil or
    melted lard
1 onion, sliced
1 pound plum tomatoes, peeled
    and chopped
1 tablespoon paprika
sugar and salt, to taste
bacon, to garnish
crusty bread, to serve

1 Wipe the green peppers, remove the cores and seeds and slice the flesh into strips.

2 Heat the oil or lard. Add the onion and cook over low heat for 5 minutes, until just softened.

3 Add the strips of pepper and cook gently for 10 minutes.

4 Add the chopped tomatoes and paprika and season to taste with a little sugar and salt.

5 Simmer the ratatouille over low heat for 20–25 minutes. Serve immediately, topped with the strips of bacon and accompanied by crusty bread.

— VARIATION —

To vary this recipe add 1 cup sliced salami, or some lightly scrambled eggs to the vegetables.

Hot Cheese Pastries

One of many recipes for cheese pastries, often served to guests with Hungarian wine.

INGREDIENTS

Makes about 30
14-ounce package puff pastry, thawed
1 large egg, beaten
4–5 ounces Liptauer cheese
   (see Cook's Tip), finely crumbled

COOK'S TIP

Hungarian *liptauer* is a cheese spread made from a white sheep's milk cheese, *liptó*, spiced with paprika, salt and various other ingredients, such as onion, caraway seeds, mustard and capers. *Liptauer* has a heady, spicy flavor. If unavailable, use feta cheese or the Romanian *brinza* instead.

1 Preheat the oven to 400°F. Roll out the puff pastry on a lightly floured surface to a 12-inch long log about ¼ inch thick. Cut the pastry in half crosswise.

2 Glaze the pastry with the beaten egg, sprinkle on the Liptauer cheese and push it lightly into the pastry. Cut the pastry into 15 6 × 1-inch strips.

3 Twist the pastry strips to form long spiral shapes. Place on a nonstick baking sheet and bake for 10–15 minutes or until golden brown. Cool on a wire rack.

Bavarian Potato Dumplings

The cuisines of Germany and Central Europe are unimaginable without dumplings, consumed in all shapes and sizes. In this version, crunchy croutons are placed in the center.

INGREDIENTS

Serves 6
3 pounds potatoes, peeled
⅔ cup semolina
1 cup whole-wheat flour
1 teaspoon salt
¼ teaspoon nutmeg
2 tablespoons sunflower oil
2 thin white bread slices, crusts
   removed, cubed
6¼ cups beef stock
freshly ground black pepper
chopped fresh flat-leaf parsley, crispy
   bacon and onion slices, to garnish
melted butter, to serve

1 Cook the potatoes in a large pan of boiling salted water for 20 minutes or until tender. Drain well, then mash and press through a sieve into a bowl. Add the semolina, flour, salt, a little pepper and the nutmeg and mix well.

2 Heat the oil in a frying pan and fry the cubes of bread until light golden brown. Drain the croutons on paper towels.

3 Divide the potato mixture into 24 balls. Press a few of the fried croutons firmly into each dumpling. Bring the stock to a boil in a large pan, add the dumplings and cook gently for 5 minutes, turning once.

4 Remove the dumplings with a slotted spoon and arrange on a warmed serving dish. Sprinkle with chopped parsley, crispy bacon and fried onion slices and serve with melted butter.

Spiced Red Cabbage

Cook this a day before serving. It is a perfect accompaniment to roast pork or game.

INGREDIENTS

Serves 6–8
3 strips bacon, diced
1 large onion, chopped
1 large red cabbage,
   evenly shredded
3 garlic cloves, crushed
1–1½ tablespoons caraway seeds
½ cup water
2 firm, ripe pears, cored and
   evenly chopped
juice of 1 lemon
2 cups red wine
3 tablespoons red wine vinegar
scant ¾ cup honey
salt and freshly ground black pepper
caraway seeds and snipped fresh chives,
   to garnish

1 Dry-fry the diced bacon in a pan over low heat for 5–10 minutes or until golden brown.

2 Stir in the onion and cook for 5 minutes or until pale golden.

3 Stir the cabbage, garlic, caraway seeds and the water into the pan. Cover and cook for 8–10 minutes.

4 Season well, then add the pears, lemon juice, red wine and vinegar. Cover and cook for 10–15 minutes. Stir in the honey.

5 If there is too much cooking liquid, remove the lid and let it reduce. The pears will have broken up in the pot. Adjust the seasoning to taste and serve sprinkled with caraway seeds and snipped fresh chives.

Spätzle

This simple pasta dish comes from Swabia in southwest Germany, where it is more popular than potatoes and is served with many savory dishes.

INGREDIENTS

Serves 4

3 cups all-purpose flour
½ teaspoon salt
2 eggs, beaten
scant 1 cup milk and water combined
1 tablespoon sunflower oil
2 tablespoons butter, melted, plus diced bacon, poached celery hearts and freshly ground black pepper, to serve

1 Sift the flour and salt into a bowl and make a well in the center. Add the eggs and enough of the milk and water to make a very soft dough.

2 Beat the dough until it develops bubbles, then stir in the oil and beat again. Bring a large pan of salted water to a boil.

3 Dampen a cutting board with water and place the dough on it. Shave off strips of the dough into the water using the broad side of a knife.

COOK'S TIP

Rinse the knife with water occasionally at Step 3, so that the dough does not stick to it. The faster you work at this stage, the lighter the texture of the *spätzle*.

4 Cook for 3 minutes, then remove the pieces with a slotted spoon. Rinse quickly in hot water, put in a warmed serving bowl and cover to keep warm. Repeat until all the dough has been used up.

5 Drizzle the melted butter on top and serve immediately, topped with diced bacon. Serve with poached celery hearts, and sprinkled with freshly ground black pepper.

DESSERTS & BAKED GOODS

Hungary, Germany and Austria are well known for an impressive range of
cakes and desserts, an enviable excellence in the art of pastry-making and an
accompanying café culture, which is famous worldwide. It is hard to know
which is the greater delight—a slice of rich Black Forest Cherry Cake or
melt-in-your-mouth Apple Strudel. Locally grown cherries, plums,
apricots and nuts are typical ingredients, while apples appear widely in
German desserts and, in particular, baked goods.

Black Forest Cherry Cake

Surprisingly, this famous and much-loved cake is a fairly recent invention. It comes from southern Germany, where Kirsch is distilled.

INGREDIENTS

Serves 12

7 ounces semi-sweet chocolate, broken into squares
1/2 cup unsalted butter
3 eggs, separated
1/2 cup dark brown sugar
3 tablespoons Kirsch
2/3 cup self-rising flour, sifted
1/2 cup ground almonds

For the filling and topping

2 1/2 ounces semi-sweet chocolate
2 1/2 ounces semi-sweet chocolate-flavored frosting
3 tablespoons Kirsch
15-ounce can pitted black cherries, drained and juice reserved
2 1/2 cups heavy cream, lightly whipped
12 fresh cherries with stalks

1 Preheat the oven to 350°F. Line the bottom of an 8-inch round cake pan with greased waxed paper. Melt the chocolate and butter in a heatproof bowl set over a pan of simmering water, stirring to mix. Remove from heat and set aside until barely warm.

2 Whisk the egg yolks and sugar in a bowl until very thick, then fold in the chocolate mixture and the Kirsch. Fold in the flour with the ground almonds. Whisk the egg whites in a greasefree bowl until stiff, then gently fold into the mixture.

3 Pour the mixture into the prepared cake pan and bake for 40 minutes or until firm to the touch.

4 Let the sponge cool in the pan for 5 minutes, then turn out and cool on a wire rack. Use a long serrated knife to cut the cake horizontally into 3 even layers.

5 Meanwhile, make the chocolate curls. Melt the chocolate and chocolate cake covering in a heatproof bowl set over a pan of simmering water, as before. Cool for 5 minutes, then pour onto a board to set. Use a potato peeler to shave off thin curls.

6 Mix the Kirsch with 6 tablespoons of the reserved cherry juice. Place the bottom layer of cake on a serving plate and sprinkle with 3 tablespoons of the Kirsch syrup.

7 Spread one-third of the whipped cream on the cake layer and sprinkle on half the cherries. Place the second layer of cake on top and repeat with another third of the Kirsch syrup and cream and the remaining cherries. Place the final cake layer on top and sprinkle the remaining Kirsch syrup over it.

8 Spread the remaining cream on top of the cake. Sprinkle on the chocolate curls and top with the fresh cherries.

Apple Strudel

This classic recipe is usually made with strudel dough, but phyllo pastry makes a good shortcut.

INGREDIENTS

Serves 8–10

1¼-pound package large sheets of phyllo pastry, thawed if frozen
½ cup unsalted butter, melted
confectioners' sugar, for dredging
cream, to serve

For the filling

2¼ pounds apples, cored, peeled and sliced
2 cups fresh bread crumbs
¼ cup unsalted butter, melted
¾ cup sugar
1 teaspoon cinnamon
generous ½ cup raisins
finely grated zest of 1 lemon

1 Preheat the oven to 350°F. For the filling, place the sliced apples in a bowl. Stir in the bread crumbs, butter, sugar, cinnamon, raisins and grated lemon zest.

2 Lay 1 or 2 sheets of pastry on a floured surface and brush with melted butter. Place another 1 or 2 sheets on top, and continue until there are 4–5 layers in all.

3 Put the apple on the pastry, with a 1-inch border all around.

4 Fold in the two shorter sides to enclose the filling, then roll up like a jelly roll. Place the strudel on a lightly buttered baking sheet.

5 Brush the pastry with the remaining butter. Bake for 30–40 minutes or until golden brown. Let cool before dusting with confectioners' sugar. Serve in thick diagonal slices.

Linzertorte

This sweet recipe was named not, as is commonly thought, after the town of Linz, but after Linzer, chef to the Archduke Charles, victor over Napoleon at Aspern in 1809. Sieve some warmed raspberry jam and brush onto the tart when cold.

INGREDIENTS

Serves 8–10
scant 1 cup butter or margarine
1 cup sugar
3 eggs, beaten
1 egg yolk
¹⁄₂ teaspoon cinnamon
grated zest of ¹⁄₂ lemon
2 cups fine cookie crumbs
1¹⁄₄ cups ground almonds
2 cups all-purpose flour, sifted
³⁄₄ cup raspberry jam
1 egg yolk, for glazing
confectioners' sugar, to decorate

1 Preheat the oven to 375°F. Cream the butter or margarine and sugar together in a mixing bowl until light and creamy. Add the eggs and egg yolk slowly, beating constantly, before adding the cinnamon and the lemon zest.

2 Stir the cookie crumbs and ground almonds into the mixture. Mix well before adding the sifted flour. Knead the pastry mixture lightly, then wrap it in plastic wrap and chill for 30 minutes.

3 Roll out two-thirds of the pastry on a lightly floured surface and use to line a 10-inch loose-bottomed tart pan. Smooth down the surface.

4 Spread the raspberry jam on the bottom of the pastry shell. Roll out the remaining pastry into a long rectangle. Cut this into strips and arrange in a lattice pattern over the jam.

5 Brush the pastry with the beaten egg yolk to glaze. Bake for 35–50 minutes or until golden brown. Let cool in the pan before transferring to a wire rack. Serve warm or cold with custard and sift on a little confectioners' sugar.

Dobos Torta

This well-known cake was first created by a chef called Jozep Dobos in the late 1880s. His famous delicacy was soon exported worldwide in his specially designed packaging. Other cooks failed to replicate this treat, so in 1906 Dobos Makers donated his recipe to the Budapest Pastry and Honey-bread Makers Guild.

INGREDIENTS

Serves 10–12
6 eggs, separated
1¼ cups confectioners' sugar, sifted
1 teaspoon vanilla sugar
generous 1 cup all-purpose flour, sifted

For the filling
3 ounces semi-sweet chocolate, broken into pieces
³/₄ cup unsalted butter
generous 1 cup confectioners' sugar
2 tablespoons vanilla sugar
1 egg

For the caramel topping
³/₄ cup sugar
2–3 tablespoons water
½ tablespoon butter, melted

1 Preheat the oven to 425°F. Whisk the egg yolks and half the confectioners' sugar together in a bowl until pale in color, thick and creamy.

2 Whisk the egg whites in a greasefree bowl until stiff; whisk in half the remaining confectioners' sugar until glossy, then fold in the vanilla sugar.

3 Fold the egg whites into the egg yolk mixture, alternating carefully with spoonfuls of the flour.

4 Line 4 baking sheets with parchment or waxed paper. Draw a 9-inch circle on each piece of paper. Lightly grease the paper and dust with flour.

5 Spread the mixture evenly on the paper circles. Bake for 10 minutes, then let cool before layering and weighing them down with a board.

6 To make the filling, melt the chocolate in a small heatproof bowl set over a pan of gently simmering water. Stir until smooth.

7 Cream the butter and confectioners' sugar together well in a bowl. Beat in the melted chocolate, vanilla sugar and egg.

8 Sandwich the 4 sponge circles together with the chocolate cream filling, then spread the remainder of the cream on the top and sides of the cake.

9 To make the caramel topping, put the sugar and water in a heavy pan and dissolve slowly over very low heat. Add the butter.

10 When the sugar has dissolved, increase the heat and cook until the mixture turns golden brown. Quickly pour the caramel onto a greased baking sheet. Let set and shatter into shards when cold. Place the pieces of caramel on top of the cake, and cut it into slices to serve.

Cheesecake with Kisel

This creamy cheesecake contrasts well with the flavor of fresh or stewed fruit, so why not try it with *kisel*? Originally a German recipe, the red-berry compôte became associated with Russia, where it was introduced by German governesses last century and is still a popular food for children and adults today.

INGREDIENTS

Serves 8–10
2 cups all-purpose flour
¹/₂ cup butter
1 tablespoon sugar
finely grated zest of ¹/₂ lemon
1 egg, beaten
sprigs of mint, to decorate

For the filling

3 cups Quark or ricotta cheese
4 eggs, separated
³/₄ cup sugar
3 tablespoons cornstarch
²/₃ cup sour cream
finely grated zest and juice of
   ¹/₂ lemon
1 teaspoon vanilla extract

For the kisel

4–4¹/₂ cups prepared berries,
   such as strawberries, raspberries,
   red currants, cherries
¹/₄ cup sugar
¹/₂ cup water
1 tablespoon arrowroot

1 Begin by making the pastry for the cheesecake. Sift the flour into a bowl. Rub in the butter until the mixture resembles fine bread crumbs. Stir in the sugar and lemon zest, then add the beaten egg and mix into a dough. Wrap in plastic wrap and chill for at least 15 minutes.

2 Roll out the pastry on a lightly floured surface and use to line the bottom and sides of a 10-inch loose-bottomed tart pan. Chill for 1 hour.

3 Put the Quark or ricotta for the filling in a fine sieve set over a bowl and let drain for 1 hour.

4 Preheat the oven to 400°F. Prick the chilled pastry with a fork, fill it with crumpled aluminum foil and bake for 5 minutes. Remove the foil and bake for another 5 minutes. Remove the pan from the oven and reduce the oven temperature to 350°F.

5 Put the drained Quark or ricotta in a bowl with the egg yolks and sugar and combine. Blend the cornstarch in a cup with a little sour cream, then add to the bowl with the remaining sour cream, the lemon zest and juice and vanilla extract. Mix well.

6 Whisk the egg whites in a greaseproof bowl until stiff, then fold into the Quark or ricotta mixture, one-third at a time. Pour the filling into the pastry and bake for 1–1¹/₄ hours, until golden and firm. Turn off the oven and leave the door ajar. Let the cheesecake cool, then chill for 2 hours.

7 To make the kisel, put the prepared fruit, sugar and water into a pan and cook over low heat until the sugar dissolves and the juices run. Remove the fruit with a slotted spoon and set aside.

8 Blend the arrowroot in a cup with a little cold water, stir into the fruit juices in the pan and bring to a boil, stirring constantly. Return the fruit to the pan and let cool, before serving it with the well-chilled cheesecake, decorated with sprigs of mint.

Apple Crêpes

These much-loved crêpes are filled with cinnamon-spiced caramelized apples.

INGREDIENTS

Serves 6
1 cup all-purpose flour
pinch of salt
2 eggs, beaten
³/₄ cup milk
½ cup water
2 tablespoons butter, melted
sunflower oil, for frying
cinnamon sugar or confectioners' sugar
   and lemon wedges, to serve (optional)

For the filling
6 tablespoons butter
3 pounds apples, cored, peeled
   and sliced
¼ cup sugar
1 teaspoon cinnamon

1 Melt the butter for the filling in a heavy frying pan. When the foam subsides, add the apple slices. Sprinkle a mixture of the sugar and cinnamon on the apples. Cook, stirring occasionally, until the apples are soft and golden brown. Set aside.

2 Sift the flour and salt into a mixing bowl and make a well in the middle. Add the eggs and gradually mix in the flour.

3 Slowly add the combined milk and the water, beating until smooth. Stir in the melted butter.

4 Heat 2 teaspoons oil in a crêpe or small frying pan. Pour in about 2 tablespoons of the batter, tilting the pan to coat the bottom evenly.

5 Cook the crêpe until the underside is golden brown, then turn over and cook the other side. Slide onto a warm plate, cover with aluminum foil and set the plate over a pan of simmering water to keep warm. Repeat with the remaining batter mixture, until it is all used up.

6 Divide the apple filling among the crêpes and roll them up. Sprinkle with cinnamon sugar or a dusting of confectioners' sugar, if desired. Serve with lemon wedges to squeeze on top.

COOK'S TIP

These crêpes taste equally good filled with sliced pears instead of apples, or a mixture of both apples and pears.

Spicy Apple Cake

Hundreds of German cakes and desserts include this versatile fruit. This moist and spicy *apfelkuchen* can be found on the menus of *Konditoreien,* coffee and tea houses, everywhere.

INGREDIENTS

Serves 12
1 cup all-purpose flour
1 cup whole-wheat flour
2 teaspoons baking powder
1 teaspoon cinnamon
½ teaspoon allspice
8 ounces apples, cored,
  peeled and chopped
6 tablespoons butter
generous ¾ cup light brown sugar
finely grated zest of 1 small orange
2 eggs, beaten
2 tablespoons milk
whipped cream dusted with
  cinnamon, to serve

For the topping
4 apples, cored and thinly sliced
juice of ½ orange
2 teaspoons sugar
3 tablespoons apricot jam,
  warmed and sieved

1 Preheat the oven to 350°F. Grease and line a 9-inch round loose-bottomed cake pan. Sift the flours, baking powder and spices together in a bowl.

2 Toss the chopped apple in 2 tablespoons of the flour mixture.

3 Cream the butter, brown sugar and orange zest together until light and fluffy. Gradually beat in the eggs, then fold in the flour mixture, the chopped apple and the milk.

4 Spoon the mixture into the cake pan and level the surface.

5 For the topping, toss the apple slices in the orange juice and set them in overlapping circles on top of the cake batter, pressing down lightly.

6 Sprinkle the sugar on top and bake for 1–1¼ hours or until risen and firm. Cover with aluminum foil if the apples brown too much.

7 Cool in the pan for 10 minutes, then remove to a wire rack. Glaze the apples with the sieved jam. Cut into wedges and serve with whipped cream, sprinkled with cinnamon.

Bavarian Cream

This light dessert is set in a fancy mold and then turned out to serve. Decorate with cream and chocolate leaves or serve simply with fresh fruit.

INGREDIENTS

Serves 6
1 vanilla bean
1¼ cups light cream
1 tablespoon powdered gelatin
3 tablespoons milk
5 egg yolks
¼ cup sugar
1¼ cups heavy cream
chocolate leaves and unsweetened
　cocoa powder, to decorate

───── COOK'S TIP ─────

If preferred, use 1 teaspoon vanilla extract instead of the vanilla bean. Omit Step 1 and whisk the vanilla extract into the egg yolks and sugar at Step 3.

1 Put the vanilla bean and light cream into a small pan. Slowly bring to a boil, then turn off the heat, cover and infuse for 30 minutes. Remove the bean—rinsed well and dried, it can be stored and used again.

2 Sprinkle the gelatin over the milk and let soften.

3 Lightly whisk the egg yolks and sugar together in a heatproof bowl. Bring the light cream almost to a boil again, then whisk into the egg mixture.

4 Set the bowl over a pan of barely simmering water and cook the custard, stirring, until it thickens enough to coat the back of a wooden spoon. Remove from heat, add the soaked gelatin and stir until dissolved.

5 Strain the custard into a clean bowl. Cover with a piece of wet waxed paper, to prevent a skin from forming and let cool.

6 Whip the heavy cream in a bowl until it just holds soft peaks, then fold it into the cooled custard.

7 Rinse individual molds or a 5-cup ring or fancy mold with water. Pour in the cream mixture and chill for at least 4 hours or until set.

8 To unmold the Bavarian cream, dip the mold right up to the rim in very hot water for about 5 seconds. Place a serving plate on top, then quickly invert the mold and remove. Decorate with chocolate leaves and a sprinkling of cocoa powder.

Plum Streusel Slices

In Saxony, in eastern Germany, cakes and fruit desserts are frequently made with this crumble or "streusel" topping. Here, plums are used as the filling in this *pflaumenstreusel*.

INGREDIENTS

Makes 14

1¹/₃ cups plums, pitted and chopped
1 tablespoon lemon juice
¹/₄ cup sugar
¹/₂ cup butter, softened
¹/₄ cup sugar
1 egg yolk
1¹/₄ cups all-purpose flour

For the topping
1¹/₄ cups all-purpose flour
¹/₂ teaspoon baking powder
6 tablespoons butter, chilled
¹/₄ cup light brown sugar
¹/₂ cup chopped hazelnuts

1 Preheat the oven to 350°F. Grease and line the bottom of an 8-inch square cake pan. Put the plums and lemon juice in a small pan and cook over low heat for 5 minutes, until soft.

2 Add the sugar to the pan and cook gently until dissolved. Simmer for 3–4 minutes, until very thick, stirring occasionally. Let cool.

3 Beat the butter and sugar together in a bowl until light and fluffy. Beat in the egg yolk, then mix in the flour to make a soft dough. Press the mixture into the bottom of the prepared cake pan. Bake for 15 minutes. Remove from the oven and spoon the cooked plums on the cake.

4 Meanwhile, to make the topping, sift the flour and baking powder into a bowl. Rub in the butter until the mixture resembles bread crumbs. Stir in the sugar and chopped nuts.

5 Sprinkle the topping mixture on the plums and press it down gently. Return the pan to the oven and bake for another 30 minutes or until the topping is lightly browned. Let cool for 15 minutes, then cut into slices. Remove from the pan when completely cold.

COOK'S TIP

Fresh apricots are a delicious alternative to plums in this recipe.

Layered Pancake Gâteau

Pancakes in Hungary were originally very basic food: made with only cornstarch and water, and then cooked over an open fire. The relative absence of ovens accounts for today's great variety of pancake recipes—both sweet and savory—in this part of the world. This unusual layered pancake gâteau is just one example of this tradition.

INGREDIENTS

Serves 6
5 eggs, separated
$^1/_4$ cup sugar
$^3/_4$ cup milk
$^1/_2$ cup self-rising flour, sifted
$^1/_4$ cup unsalted butter, melted
$^3/_4$ cup sour cream
sifted confectioners' sugar, for dredging
lemon wedges, to serve

For the filling
3 eggs, separated
$^1/_4$ cup confectioners' sugar, sifted
grated zest of 1 lemon
$^1/_2$ teaspoon vanilla sugar
1 cup ground almonds

1 Preheat the oven to 400°F. Grease and line a deep 8–9-inch springform cake pan. Whisk the egg yolks and sugar together in a bowl until thick and creamy, before whisking in the milk.

2 Whisk the egg whites in a greasefree bowl until stiff, then fold into the batter mixture, alternating with spoonfuls of the flour and half the melted butter.

3 Take a frying pan as close to the size of your prepared cake pan as possible, and lightly grease the pan with a little of the remaining melted butter. Tilt to cover the surface.

4 Put one-quarter of the batter into the frying pan. Fry the thick pancake on each side until golden brown, then slide it into the prepared cake pan. Use up the batter to make 3 more pancakes in the same way and set them aside while you make the filling.

5 For the filling, whisk the egg yolks in a bowl with the confectioners' sugar until thick and creamy. Stir in the grated lemon zest and the vanilla sugar.

6 Whisk the egg whites in a separate bowl, then fold them into the egg yolk mixture, before adding the ground almonds. Combine well.

7 Spread one-third of the mixture on top of the first pancake.

8 Repeat twice more with the second and third pancakes, then top with the final pancake.

9 Spread the sour cream on top and bake for 20–25 minutes or until the top is pale golden brown.

10 Keep in the pan for 10 minutes before removing the lining paper. Serve warm, cut into wedges, generously dusted with confectioners' sugar and accompanied by lemon wedges.

Stewed Fruit

This recipe is good for using up odd or small amount of fresh fruit. Serve the medley of fruit well chilled.

INGREDIENTS

Serves 6

½–¾ cup sugar, depending on the tartness of the fruit
1 cup cold water
juice and strip of zest from ½ lemon
1 cinnamon stick, broken in half
2 pounds prepared fruit, such as cored, peeled and sliced apples, pears, quince; pitted plums, peaches, apricots; trimmed gooseberries; cranberries, blueberries, strawberries
2 tablespoons arrowroot
sugar and cream (optional), to serve

1 Put the sugar and water in a stainless steel pan and bring to a boil. Add the lemon juice and zest and the two pieces of cinnamon stick. Cook for 1 minute.

2 Add the prepared fruit to the pan and cook for just 2–3 minutes. Remove the fruit and cinnamon stick with a slotted spoon.

3 Blend the arrowroot with a little cold water, stir into the fruit juices and bring to a boil. Return the fruit to the saucepan and let it cool before chilling. Discard the cinnamon stick.

4 Serve the fruit sprinkled with sugar, and with whipped cream, if desired.

Sweet Cheese Dumplings

The most famous cheese dumplings come from Czech countries, but they are popular elsewhere, as this Austrian version shows. Sweet and savory versions combined together, such as this one here, are known as *mehlspeisen*.

INGREDIENTS

Serves 4–6

3 tablespoons unsalted butter
3 eggs, separated
2 cups ricotta cheese
⅓ cup semolina
1 heavy double cream
1–2 tablespoons all-purpose flour
sifted confectioners' sugar and sprigs of mint, to decorate

1 Cream the butter and beat in the egg yolks, one at a time. Stir in the ricotta cheese, semolina and cream. Mix well, cover and let stand for 45 minutes.

2 Whisk the egg whites in a greasefree bowl until stiff, then carefully fold into the ricotta cheese mixture together with the flour.

3 Boil a very large pan of salted water. Scoop spoonfuls of mixture about the size of a plum and roll into ovals or balls with damp hands.

4 Drop the dumplings into the boiling water and simmer for 6–7 minutes. Remove with a slotted spoon and drain well. Serve warm, dredged liberally with confectioners' sugar and decorated with sprigs of mint.

Nut Squares

This light and delicious Czech recipe is good with coffee in the morning or served as a dessert.

INGREDIENTS

Makes about 24

1 cup unsalted butter
generous 1 cup sugar
3 egg yolks
1½ cups all-purpose flour, sifted
4 eggs, beaten
1½ cups ground walnuts
scant ⅓ cup day-old white bread crumbs
unsweetened cocoa powder for sprinkling

For the topping

3 egg whites
¾ cup sugar
1 cup ground walnuts
½ cup raisins, chopped
¼ cup unsweetened cocoa powder, sifted

1 Preheat the oven to 300°F. Grease and line a 11 × 7 × 1½-inch jelly roll pan.

2 Cream the butter and sugar together until pale and fluffy, then beat in the egg yolks.

3 Fold half the flour into the mixture, then beat in the whole eggs slowly before stirring in the remaining flour and the walnuts.

4 Sprinkle the prepared jelly roll pan with the bread crumbs before spooning in the walnut mixture. Level the mixture with a round-bladed knife. Bake for 30–35 minutes or until cooked and pale golden brown.

5 Meanwhile, make the topping. Whisk the egg whites in a greasefree bowl until stiff. Slowly whisk in the sugar until glossy, before folding in the walnuts, raisins and cocoa powder.

6 Spread the topping mixture on the cooked bottom and cook for another 15 minutes. Let cool in the pan. When cold, peel off the lining paper. Cut into squares or fingers, and sprinkle with cocoa powder.

Lebkuchen

These sweet and spicy cakes, a specialty of Nuremberg in Bavaria, are traditionally baked at Christmas. In German, their name means "cake of life."

INGREDIENTS

Makes 20

1 cup blanched almonds, finely chopped
$^1/_3$ cup candied orange peel, finely chopped
finely grated zest of $^1/_2$ lemon
3 cardamom pods
1 teaspoon cinnamon
$^1/_4$ teaspoon nutmeg
$^1/_4$ teaspoon ground cloves
2 eggs
scant $^3/_4$ cup sugar
$1^1/_4$ cups all-purpose flour
$^1/_2$ teaspoon baking powder
rice paper (optional)

For the icing

$^1/_2$ egg white
$^3/_4$ cup confectioners' sugar, sifted
1 teaspoon white rum

1 Preheat the oven to 350°F. Set aside some of the blanched almonds for sprinkling and put the remainder in a bowl with the candied orange peel and lemon zest.

3 Whisk the eggs and sugar in a mixing bowl until thick and foamy. Sift in the flour and baking powder, then gently fold into the eggs before adding to the nut and spice mixture.

5 Bake for 20 minutes, until golden. Let cool for a few minutes, then break off the surplus rice paper or remove the cookies from the baking parchment and cool on a wire rack.

2 Remove the black seeds from the cardamom pods and crush using a mortar and pestle. Add to the bowl with the cinnamon, nutmeg and cloves and mix well.

4 Spoon spoonfuls of the mixture onto sheets of rice paper, if using, or baking parchment placed on baking sheets, allowing room for the mixture to spread. Sprinkle on the reserved almonds.

6 Put the egg white for the icing in a bowl and lightly whisk with a fork. Stir in a little of the confectioners' sugar at a time, then add the rum. Drizzle on the *lebkuchen* and let set. Store in a tin for 2 weeks before serving.

Stollen

Dating from the 12th century, and symbolizing the Holy Child wrapped in cloth, this traditional German Christmas cake is made from a rich yeast dough with marzipan and dried fruits.

INGREDIENTS

Serves 12

3 cups all-purpose flour
pinch of salt
¼ cup sugar
2 teaspoons active dry yeast
⅔ cup milk
½ cup butter
1 egg, beaten
1 cup mixed dried fruit
¼ cup candied cherries, quartered
½ cup blanched almonds, chopped
finely grated zest of 1 lemon
1 cup marzipan
confectioners' sugar, for dredging

1 Sift the flour, salt and sugar. Stir in the yeast. Make a well in the center. Over low heat, gently melt the milk and butter. Cool, then mix with the egg into the sifted dry ingredients.

2 Turn out the dough onto a lightly floured surface and knead for 10 minutes, until smooth and elastic. Put in a clean bowl, cover with plastic wrap and set in a warm place to rise for about 1 hour or until doubled in size.

3 On a lightly floured surface, knead in the dried fruit, cherries, almonds and lemon zest.

4 Roll out the dough to a rectangle, about 10 × 8 inches.

5 Roll the marzipan into a sausage, slightly shorter than the dough. Place on the dough in the middle. Enclose the paste in dough.

6 Put seam side down on a greased baking sheet. Cover with oiled plastic wrap and set in a warm place to rise for about 40 minutes, or until doubled in size. Preheat the oven to 375°F.

7 Bake the stollen for 30–35 minutes or until golden and hollow sounding when tapped on the underside. Let cool on a wire rack. Serve thickly dusted with confectioners' sugar.

Black Bread

Black bread is eaten throughout Eastern Europe. This German yeastless version has a dense texture similar to that of pumpernickel and is steamed rather than baked. Empty food cans are perfect for producing bread in the traditional round shape.

INGREDIENTS

Makes 2 loaves

½ cup rye flour
⅓ cup all-purpose flour
¾ teaspoon baking powder
½ teaspoon salt
¼ teaspoon cinnamon
¼ teaspoon nutmeg
⅓ cup fine semolina
4 tablespoons molasses
scant 1 cup buttermilk
cherry jam, sour cream or crème fraîche and a sprinkling of ground allspice, to serve

1 Grease and line 2 14-ounce food cans. Sift the flours, baking powder, salt and spices into a large bowl. Stir in the semolina.

COOK'S TIP

If you cannot get buttermilk, use ordinary milk instead, first sour with 1 teaspoon lemon juice.

2 Add the molasses and buttermilk and mix thoroughly.

3 Divide the mixture between 2 cans, then cover each with a double layer of greased pleated aluminum foil.

4 Place the cans on a trivet in a large pan and pour in enough hot water to come halfway up the sides. Cover tightly and steam for 2 hours, checking the water level occasionally.

5 Carefully remove the cans from the steamer. Turn the bread out onto a wire rack and cool completely. Wrap in foil and use within 1 week.

6 Serve the bread in slices, spread with cherry jam, topped with a spoonful of sour cream or crème fraîche and a sprinkling of allspice.

ROMANIA, BULGARIA
AND THE
EAST ADRIATIC

The recipes from this region abound with examples of colorful, flavorful cooking. Mediterranean, Middle Eastern and Central European influences combine to produce a collection that is full of surprises, from fiery chiles to the delicacy of rose petals.

INGREDIENTS

Left, from front: tomatoes, capsicum, large fresh chiles, eggplant, zucchini, cucumber and green beans.

Below, from the back: salmon, grey mullet, octopus, sea bass, mackerel, whitebait and trout.

VEGETABLES

Southern vegetables such as peppers, eggplant, zucchini and tomatoes all feature strongly in Balkan cuisine, together with more northerly onions and cabbage. Piquant stews of peppers and eggplant with garlic, vinegar and oil are used as relishes or served with bread. Romanian grilled meat dishes are often accompanied by pickled vegetables, such as cucumbers or chiles.

FISH

The predominant inland fish, that might once have been caught in the Danube, are carp, river trout, sturgeon and sterlet, pike, perch, bream and freshwater crayfish. Traditionally, excellent catfish comes from the Danube delta, while on the Adriatic coast squid and octopus are caught, as well as mackerel, sardines, tuna and white fish, such as sea bass and gilt-head bream. Species found in the Black Sea include scad, small oily fish that resemble whitebait and are fried in batter and eaten whole.

DAIRY PRODUCTS

Kashkaval, properly made from sheep's milk, is the general name for the yellow cheese produced in the Balkans. Depending on how it is made, it can be piquant, or rubbery and bland. It is often available at Greek, Middle Eastern and Cypriot delicatessens and is excellent for grating, toasting and frying. A good substitute is Italian pecorino. *Brinza* is the Romanian equivalent of the brine cheese used throughout East European cooking, for which feta may be substituted.

Bulgarian yogurt has become a legendary source of health and longevity, but it may be replaced by any good quality live organic yogurt. It is the key ingredient in a cold cucumber soup of the region. A unique Serbian specialty is *kaimak*, which is thick cream made from boiled milk.

Far left, clockwise from left: red kidney beans, mamaliga, *white beans and black kidney beans.*

Left, clockwise from left: peaches, lemons, oranges, apricots, cherries, pistachios and shelled walnuts.

GRAINS AND PULSES

Mamaliga, cooked cornmeal used as an accompaniment to meat dishes, or with cheese or bacon, is a distinctive Romanian specialty, although it is now encountered less often than it was 50 years ago. The tradition of making this bright yellow porridge came to Europe from the New World in the 16th century, and it has remained a favorite also with Italians, who call it polenta.

The handground cornmeal was cooked in water over an open fire until it was so thick that it could be sliced like bread when cool. The tools for making *mamaliga*, an iron cauldron and a large wooden stirring stick, are prized decorative objects.

Red and black kidney beans and white or lima beans are widely used in soups.

FRUIT AND NUTS

Cherries, peaches, apricots, figs and watermelons are widely enjoyed when in season. Chestnuts form an important part of baking in some regions such as Slovenia, as do apples, and Balkan pastries of all kinds are filled with the walnuts and hazelnuts that grow in abundance. Walnuts are also used to thicken the typical cold soups.

HERBS, SPICES AND OTHER FLAVORINGS

Fresh herbs such as parsley, thyme, tarragon, basil, savory, mint and dill are widely used in the Balkans—in salads, soups and casseroles. Chili peppers give a typical fire to Balkan cooking. A more unusual herb, lovage, comparable with the taste of celery leaves, is typically used in Romanian cooking, especially in lamb soup. It is not difficult to buy and is also easily grown at home. The Balkan countries also have a taste for soups soured with lemon juice or a dash of vinegar.

Rose water and rose petals flavor and decorate Bulgarian desserts, such as rice puddings. The Valley of the Roses, which crosses Bulgaria from west to east, was planted by the Turks in the 17th century; since then, it has become the home of the precious oil called rose attar, and the basis of a small industry in soap and rose liqueur.

Right, clockwise from front left: fresh chiles, vinegar, olive oil, fresh herbs, rose water and petals, dried thyme, Kashkaval *sheep's milk cheese, yogurt and olives (center).*

DRINKS

Coffee of the strong, thick Turkish variety is widely loved throughout the Balkans and east Adriatic countries. It is often served with an accompanying sweet such as *lokum* (Turkish delight).

Maraschino, made of cherries, *travarica*, flavored with herbs, and *slivovica* (slivowicz), a plum brandy, are all popular liqueurs in the countries of the former Yugoslavia. The Romanian national spirit is *tuica*, a very potent plum eau de vie or brandy. Bulgaria produces a rose liqueur and also one of aniseed, called *mastica*, which is similar to the Greek raki.

SOUPS AND APPETIZERS

East Europeans are renowned for their hospitality, and homemade soup is often to be found on the stove, ready for eating at any time of the day. Sour-flavored soups, called chorbas, are a traditional specialty of this region, as is the unusual combination of fruit and vegetables in their soups.

Meze, or appetizers, reflect the typical flavors and ingredients of the region, such as local cheeses, fresh fish and shellfish, tomatoes, capsicums and herbs and spices. Served hot or cold, they are the perfect beginning to a meal.

Cold Cucumber and Yogurt Soup with Walnuts

A refreshing cold soup, using a classic combination of cucumber and yogurt, typical of the area.

INGREDIENTS

Serves 5–6
1 cucumber
4 garlic cloves
¹⁄₂ teaspoon salt
³⁄₄ cup walnut pieces
1¹⁄₂ ounces day-old bread,
  torn into pieces
2 tablespoons walnut or sunflower oil
1²⁄₃ cups cow's or sheep's milk yogurt
¹⁄₂ cup cold water or chilled still
  mineral water
1–2 teaspoons lemon juice

For the garnish
scant ¹⁄₂ cup walnuts, coarsely chopped
1¹⁄₂ tablespoons olive oil
sprigs of fresh dill

1 Cut the cucumber in half and peel one half of it. Dice the cucumber flesh and set aside.

2 Using a large mortar and pestle, crush the garlic and salt together well; add the walnuts and bread.

— COOK'S TIP —

If you prefer your soup smooth, purée it in a food processor or blender before serving.

3 When the mixture is smooth, add the walnut or sunflower oil slowly and combine well.

4 Transfer the mixture into a large bowl and beat in the yogurt and diced cucumber.

5 Add the cold water or mineral water and lemon juice to taste.

6 Pour the soup into chilled soup bowls to serve. Garnish with the coarsely chopped walnuts, a little olive oil drizzled on the nuts and sprigs of fresh dill.

Bulgarian Sour Lamb Soup

This soup—a variation on the basic traditional sour soup, or *chorba*—has long been associated with Bulgaria. This recipe uses lamb, and pork and poultry are also popular.

INGREDIENTS

Serves 4–5

2 tablespoons oil
1 pound lean lamb,
  trimmed and cubed
1 onion, diced
2 tablespoons all-purpose flour
1 tablespoon paprika
4 cups hot lamb stock
3 parsley sprigs
4 scallions
4 dill sprigs
scant ¹/₄ cup long-grain rice
2 eggs, beaten
2–3 tablespoons or more vinegar
  or lemon juice
salt and freshly ground black pepper
crusty bread, to serve

For the garnish
2 tablespoons butter, melted
1 teaspoon paprika
a little parsley or lovage and dill

1 In a large pan, heat the oil and then brown the meat. Add the onion and cook until it has softened.

2 Sprinkle in the flour and paprika. Stir well, add the stock and cook for 10 minutes.

3 Tie the parsley, scallions and dill together with string and add to the pan with the rice and a little salt and pepper. Bring to a boil, then simmer for 30–40 minutes or until the lamb is tender.

COOK'S TIP

Do not reheat this soup since the eggs could become scrambled.

4 Remove the pan from heat then add the beaten eggs, stirring continuously. Add the vinegar or lemon juice. Remove and discard the tied herbs and season to taste.

5 For the garnish, melt the butter and paprika together in a small pan. Ladle the soup into warmed serving bowls. Garnish with herbs and a little red paprika butter. Serve with thick chunks of bread.

Apple Soup

Romania has vast fruit orchards, and this soup is a delicious result of that natural resource.

INGREDIENTS

Serves 6
1 kohlrabi
3 carrots
2 celery stalks
1 green bell pepper, seeded
2 tomatoes
3 tablespoons oil
8 cups chicken stock
6 large green apples
3 tablespoons all-purpose flour
²/₃ cup heavy cream
1 tablespoon granulated sugar
2–3 tablespoons lemon juice
salt and freshly ground black pepper
lemon wedges and crusty bread,
   to serve

1 Dice the kohlrabi, carrots, celery, green pepper and tomatoes in a large pan, add the oil and cook for 5–6 minutes, until just softened.

2 Pour in the chicken stock, bring to a boil, then reduce the heat and simmer for 45 minutes.

3 Meanwhile, peel, core and dice the apples, then add to the pan and simmer for another 15 minutes.

4 In a bowl, combine the flour and heavy cream, then pour slowly into the soup, stirring well, and bring to a boil. Add the sugar and lemon juice before seasoning to taste. Serve immediately, accompanied by lemon wedges and crusty bread.

Chickpea Soup

Chickpeas form part of the staple diet in the Balkans, used either whole or ground. This soup is economical to make, and various spicy sausages may be added to give extra flavor.

INGREDIENTS

Serves 4–6
3¹/₂ cups chickpeas, rinsed and
   drained well
8 cups chicken or vegetable stock
3 large waxy potatoes, peeled and cut
   into bite-size chunks
¹/₄ cup olive oil
8 ounces spinach leaves, washed and
   well-drained
salt and freshly ground black pepper

1 Place the chickpeas in a bowl of cold water and let sit overnight. The next day, drain them well and place in a large pan with the stock.

2 Bring to a boil, then reduce the heat and cook gently for about 55 minutes. Add the potatoes, olive oil and seasoning, and cook for 20 minutes.

3 Five minutes before the end of cooking, add the spinach. Serve the soup in warmed soup bowls.

Lamb Meatball Soup with Vegetables

This family recipe is an ideal way to use up leftover vegetables.

INGREDIENTS

Serves 4
4 cups lamb stock
1 onion, finely chopped
2 carrots, finely sliced
½ celeriac, finely diced
¾ cup frozen peas
2 ounces green beans,
    cut into 1-inch pieces
3 tomatoes, seeded and chopped
1 red bell pepper, seeded and finely diced
1 potato, coarsely diced
2 lemons, sliced
salt and freshly ground black pepper
crusty bread, to serve

For the meatballs
8 ounces very lean ground lamb
¼ cup short-grain rice
2 tablespoons chopped fresh parsley
all-purpose flour, for coating
salt and freshly ground black pepper

1 Put the stock, all of the vegetables, the slices of lemon and a little seasoning in a large pan. Bring to a boil, then reduce the heat and simmer for 15–20 minutes.

2 Meanwhile, for the meatballs, combine the ground meat, rice and parsley together in a bowl and season well.

3 Roll the mixture into small balls, roughly the size of walnuts and toss them in the flour.

4 Drop the meatballs into the soup and simmer gently for 25–30 minutes, stirring occasionally, to prevent the meatballs from sticking. Adjust the seasoning to taste and serve the soup in warmed serving bowls, accompanied by crusty bread.

Fried Bell Peppers with Cheese

This traditional Bulgarian dish may vary slightly from place to place in the Balkan area, but it is usually served as an appetizer or light snack. The peppers may be red, yellow or green.

INGREDIENTS

Serves 2–4
4 long bell peppers
$\frac{1}{2}$ cup all-purpose flour, seasoned
1 egg, beaten
olive oil, for shallow-frying
cucumber and tomato salad,
  to serve

For the filling
1 egg, beaten
scant $\frac{1}{2}$ cup feta cheese, finely
  crumbled
2 tablespoons chopped fresh parsley
1 small chile, seeded and
  finely chopped

1 Slit open the peppers lengthwise, enabling you to scoop out the seeds and remove the cores, but leaving the peppers in one piece.

2 Carefully open the peppers and place under a preheated broiler, skin-side facing up. Cook until the skin is charred and blackened. Place the peppers on a plate, cover with plastic wrap and let sit for 10 minutes.

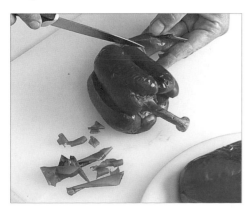

3 Using a sharp knife, carefully peel off the skin from the peppers.

4 In a bowl, combine all the filling ingredients. Divide evenly among the four peppers.

5 Reshape the peppers to look whole. Dip them into the seasoned flour, then the egg, then the flour

6 Fry the peppers gently in a little olive oil for 6–8 minutes, turning once, or until golden brown and the filling is set. Drain the peppers on paper towels before serving with a cucumber and tomato salad.

Bessarabian Crêpes

Bessarabia is the historical name for modern Moldova, in Romania, the source for these spinach and cheese crêpes.

INGREDIENTS

Serves 4–6
4 eggs, beaten
3 tablespoons butter, melted
1 cup light cream
1 cup seltzer water
1½ cups all-purpose flour, sifted
pinch of salt
1 egg white, lightly beaten
oil, for frying

For the filling
1½ cups feta cheese, crumbled
⅔ cup Parmesan
    cheese, grated
3 tablespoons butter
1 garlic clove, crushed
1 pound frozen spinach, thawed
shavings of Parmesan, to garnish

1 Blend the eggs, butter, cream and water in a food processor or blender. With the motor running, spoon the flour and salt through the feeder tube until the batter mixture is smooth and lump free. Let stand for 15 minutes to rest, loosely covered with plastic wrap.

2 Lightly grease a 5–6-inch nonstick frying pan and place over medium heat. When hot, pour in 3–4 tablespoons of the batter, tilting the pan to spread the mixture thinly.

3 Cook for 1½–2 minutes or until the underside of the crêpe is pale golden brown, then turn over and cook the other side.

4 Repeat the process until all the batter has been used, stacking the crêpes on a warm plate as you go.

5 For the filling, in a clean bowl combine the crumbled feta and Parmesan cheese, the butter and garlic clove. Thoroughly stir in the squeeze-dried spinach.

6 Place 2–3 tablespoons of the filling mixture on the center of each crêpe. Brush a little egg white around the outer edges of the crêpes and then fold them over. Press the edges down well to seal.

7 Fry the crêpes in a little oil on both sides, turning gently, until they are golden brown and the filling is hot. Serve immediately, garnished with Parmesan shavings.

Cheese Scrolls

These delicious Bulgarian cheese savories are traditionally served warm as a first course, or else as a snack in cafés, restaurants and homes at any time of the day.

INGREDIENTS

Makes 14–16

2 cups feta cheese, well drained and finely crumbled
6 tablespoons plain yogurt
2 eggs, beaten
14–16 16 × 12-inch sheets ready-made phyllo pastry, thawed if frozen
1 cup unsalted butter, melted
sea salt and chopped scallions, to garnish

1 Preheat the oven to 400°F. In a large bowl combine the feta cheese, yogurt and eggs, beating well until the mixture is smooth.

2 Fit a piping bag with a large ½-inch plain round nozzle and fill with half of the cheese mixture.

COOK'S TIP

If possible, use the locally made sheep's cheese, *bryndza*. Made throughout Eastern Europe, it is a subtly-flavored, crumbly and moist cheese that resembles feta, but it is not as salty. It is increasingly available at Middle Eastern or Cypriot food stores.

3 Lay out one sheet of pastry, fold into a 12 × 8-inch rectangle and brush with a little melted butter. Along one long edge pipe the cheese mixture ¼ inch away from the edge.

4 Roll up the pastry to form a sausage shape and tuck in each end, to prevent the filling from escaping. Brush with more melted butter.

5 Form the "sausage" into a tight "S" or a crescent shape. Repeat with the remaining ingredients, refilling the piping bag as necessary.

6 Arrange the scrolls on a buttered baking sheet and sprinkle with a little sea salt and chopped scallions. Bake for 20 minutes or until golden brown and crispy. Cool on a wire rack before serving.

Eggplant and Bell Pepper Spread

This spread is typical of rich, cooked vegetable mixtures, which can be used on breads, as a dip or with grilled meat.

INGREDIENTS

Serves 6–8
1½ pounds eggplant,
  halved lengthways
2 green bell peppers,
  seeded and quartered
3 tablespoons olive oil
2 firm ripe tomatoes, halved, seeded
  and finely chopped
3 tablespoons chopped fresh parsley
  or coriander
2 garlic cloves, crushed
2 tablespoons red wine vinegar
lemon juice, to taste
salt and freshly ground black pepper
sprigs of parsley or cilantro, to garnish
dark rye bread and lemon wedges,
  to serve

1 Place the eggplant and peppers under a preheated broiler, skin-sides facing up, and cook until the skin blisters and chars. Turn the vegetables over and cook for another 3 minutes. Place in a plastic bag and let sit for 10 minutes.

2 Peel off the blackened skin and purée the eggplant and pepper flesh in a food processor.

3 With the motor running, pour the olive oil in a continuous stream, through the feeder tube.

4 Carefully remove the blade and stir in the chopped tomatoes, parsley or cilantro, garlic, vinegar and lemon juice. Season to taste, garnish with fresh parsley or cilantro and serve with dark rye bread and wedges of lemon.

Tarama

This well-known hors d'oeuvre is made from hard fish roes, generally from grey mullet or cod, to which salt has been added as a preservative.

INGREDIENTS

Serves 4–6
8 tablespoons smoked tarama
  or cod's roe
1 tablespoon lemon juice
¾ cup olive oil,
  plus a little extra for drizzling
¾ ounces finely grated onion
1–1½ tablespoons boiling water
paprika, for sprinkling
black olives and celery leaves,
  to garnish
toast, to serve

1 Soak the cod's roe in cold water for 2 hours. Drain, then peel off any outer skin and membrane from the roe and discard it. Process the roe in a food processor or blender at a low speed.

2 Add the lemon juice and then, with the motor still running, slowly add the olive oil through the feeder tube.

3 Once thickened, beat in the onion and water. Spoon into a serving bowl and chill well. Sprinkle with a little paprika. Garnish with the olives and celery leaves. Drizzle with a little oil and serve with toasted bread.

Grilled Bell Pepper Salad

This Romanian dish, *Salata de Ardei*, is generally served as an appetizer (*meze*), or as a dish to accompany cold meats. *Meze* are served on a flat dish divided into different sections so that another three or four complementary *meze* may be added, such as diced salami, feta cheese, olives or pickle.

INGREDIENTS

Serves 4

8 long green and/or orange
   bell peppers
1 garlic clove, crushed
5 tablespoons olive oil
¼ cup wine vinegar
4 tomatoes, sliced
1 red onion, thinly sliced
freshly ground black pepper
sprigs of cilantro, to garnish
black bread, to serve

1 Cut the peppers into quarters, discarding the cores, seeds and tops. Place under a preheated broiler, skin-side facing up, and cook until the skin chars and blisters.

--- COOK'S TIP ---

The long peppers used in this recipe are increasingly available, but if you cannot find them, use small ordinary peppers.

2 Place the peppers in a plastic bag and set aside for 15 minutes.

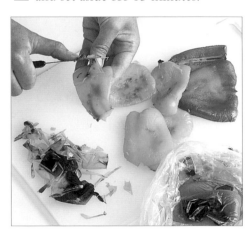

3 Remove the peppers from the bag and scrape off the skins using a sharp knife.

4 Blend the garlic, olive oil and vinegar. Arrange the peppers, tomatoes and onion on four serving plates and pour on the garlic dressing. Season, garnish with sprigs of cilantro and serve with black bread.

Octopus Salad

The Adriatic Sea separates Italy and the former Yugoslavian countries, which accounts for many of the similarities between their cuisines—particularly in their fondness for fresh fish and shellfish, olives, oil and vinegar.

INGREDIENTS

Serves 4–6

2 pounds baby octopus or squid, skinned
3/4 cup olive oil
2 tablespoons white wine vinegar
2 tablespoons chopped fresh parsley or cilantro
12 black olives, stoned
2 shallots, thinly sliced
1 red onion, thinly sliced
salt and freshly ground black pepper
sprigs of cilantro, to garnish
8–12 Romaine lettuce leaves and lemon wedges, to serve

1 In a large saucepan, boil the octopus or squid in salted water for 20–25 minutes or until just soft. Strain and let to cool before covering and chilling for 45 minutes.

--- COOK'S TIP ---

Take care not to overcook the octopus or squid or it will become tough and rubbery.

2 Cut the tentacles from the body and head, then chop all the flesh into even pieces, slicing across the thick part of the tentacles and following the direction of the suckers.

3 In a bowl, combine the olive oil and white wine vinegar.

4 Add the parsley, olives, shallots, octopus and red onion to the bowl. Season to taste and toss well.

5 Arrange the octopus on a bed of lettuce, garnish with cilantro and serve with lemon wedges.

MEAT AND POULTRY

Lamb has long reigned supreme throughout the Balkans, and it provides many delicious dishes, such as classic kebabs and slowly cooked casseroles and stews, and pastry-encased whole cuts for special occasions.

Balkan cooking has been shaped by many influences, producing an amazing variety. This recipe for Pork Schnitzel, combining sour cream with pork, is reminiscent of its northern neighbors Hungary and Austria, and the addition of spices to Rolled Beef gives that dish a distinctive Turkish flavor.

Lamb-stuffed Squash

This recipe is ideal for using any leftover cooked meat and rice.

INGREDIENTS

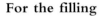

Serves 6 as a main course,
*   12 as an appetizer*
6 acorn squash, halved
3 tablespoons lemon juice
2 tablespoons butter
2 tablespoons all-purpose flour
1 cup whipping cream
³/₄ cup passata
½ cup feta cheese, crumbled, and basil
    leaves, to garnish, plus extra, to serve

For the filling

12–16 ounces cooked lean lamb
6 ounces cooked long-grain rice
2 tablespoons butter, melted
½ cup fresh bread crumbs
¼ cup milk
2 tablespoons finely grated onion
2 tablespoons chopped fresh parsley
2 eggs, beaten
salt and freshly ground black pepper

1 Preheat the oven to 350°F. Trim the bottoms of the squash, if necessary, so that they will stand up securely. Using a teaspoon, remove the insides of the squash, taking care not to cut through the outer skin or bottom. Leave about ½ inch of flesh at the bottom.

2 Blanch the squash in boiling water with the lemon juice for 2–3 minutes, then plunge them into cold water. Drain well and let cool.

3 Meanwhile, make the filling by combining the cooked lamb and rice, the butter, bread crumbs, milk, onion, parsley, eggs and seasoning. Place the squash in a lightly greased ovenproof dish, and fill with the lamb mixture.

4 To make the sauce, put the butter and flour in a pan. Whisk in the cream and bring to a boil, whisking constantly. Cook for 1–2 minutes, until thickened, then season well. Pour the sauce onto the prepared squash, then pour on the passata.

5 Bake the squash for 25–30 minutes. Drizzle them with a little of the sauce, and sprinkle with feta cheese and basil leaves. Pass any extra sauce, feta cheese and basil.

COOK'S TIP

You could use a thick zucchini instead of the acorn squash, removing the seeds in the same way.

Bulgarian Lamb in Pastry

This is an impressive dish to serve on special occasions. Skim the meat juices, bring them back to a boil and serve as a gravy with the lamb.

INGREDIENTS

Serves 6–8
3½-pound leg of lamb, boned
3 tablespoons butter
½ teaspoon each dried thyme, basil
   and oregano
2 garlic cloves, crushed
3 tablespoons lemon juice
salt, for sprinkling
1 egg, beaten, for sealing and glazing
1 oregano or marjoram sprig,
   to garnish

For the pastry
4 cups all-purpose flour, sifted
generous 1 cup chilled butter, diced
⅔–1 cup ice water

1 Preheat the oven to 375°F. To make the pastry, place the flour and butter into a food processor or blender and process until the mixture resembles fine bread crumbs. Add enough ice water to make a soft, but not sticky, dough. Knead gently and form into a ball. Wrap in plastic wrap and refrigerate for 1–2 hours.

2 Meanwhile, put the lamb in a roasting pan, tie it with string and cut 20 small holes in the meat, with a sharp, narrow knife.

3 Cream the butter, dried herbs, garlic and lemon juice and use to fill the small cuts in the lamb. Sprinkle the lamb with salt.

4 Cook the lamb in a roasting pan for about 1 hour, then let cool. Remove the string.

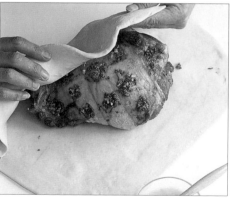

5 Roll out the pastry on a lightly floured surface until large enough to wrap around the lamb in one piece. Seal the pastry edges with a little of the egg and place in a clean pan.

6 With any remaining scraps of pastry, make leaves or other shapes to decorate the pastry. Brush with more of the egg. Return to the oven and bake for another 30–45 minutes. Serve hot, in slices, accompanied by the gravy from the meat juices, and garnished with a sprig of oregano or marjoram.

Meatloaf

Like many Serbian recipes, this dish is easy to make, requiring nothing more than good quality meat and plenty of fresh herbs.

INGREDIENTS

Serves 4–6

8 strips bacon
2 strips bacon, diced
1 onion, finely chopped
2 garlic cloves, crushed
2 cups fresh bread crumbs
6 tablespoons milk
1 pound lean ground beef
1 pound lean ground pork
½ teaspoon chopped fresh thyme
2 tablespoons chopped fresh parsley
2 eggs, beaten
salt and freshly ground black pepper
herbed mashed potatoes and carrots, to serve

1 Preheat the oven to 400°F. Line a 7½-cup buttered loaf pan with the bacon. Stretch the bacon strips with the back of a knife, if necessary, to completely line the base and edges of the pan.

2 Dry-fry the diced bacon in a large frying pan until almost crisp. Stir in the onion and garlic and sauté for another 2–3 minutes, until they are soft and a pale golden brown.

3 In a large bowl, soak the bread crumbs in the milk for 5 minutes or until all the milk is absorbed.

4 Add the ground meats, bacon, onion, garlic, herbs and eggs to the bread crumbs. Season and mix well.

5 Spoon the mixture into the loaf pan. Level the top and cover the pan with aluminum foil. Bake for about 1½ hours. Turn out and serve in slices, with herbed mashed potatoes and carrots.

Pork with Sauerkraut

The presence of sauerkraut and mustard suggests links with Central European cuisines, but the presence of chiles is a purely southern touch.

INGREDIENTS

Serves 4

1 pound lean pork or veal, diced
¼ cup vegetable oil or melted lard
½ teaspoon paprika
14 ounces sauerkraut, drained and rinsed well
2 fresh red chiles
6 tablespoons pork stock
salt and freshly ground black pepper
¼ cup sour cream
coarse-grain mustard, paprika and sage leaves, to garnish
crusty bread, to serve

1 In a heavy frying pan, cook the pork or veal in the oil until browned on all sides.

2 Add the paprika and shredded sauerkraut. Stir well and transfer to a flameproof casserole.

3 Halve the chiles and remove the seeds before burying the chiles in the middle of the casserole.

4 Add the stock to the casserole. Cover tightly and cook over low heat for 1–1½ hours, stirring occasionally to prevent it from sticking.

5 Remove the chiles, if desired, and season to taste before serving. Spoon on the sour cream and spoonfuls of mustard, sprinkle with paprika and garnish with sage leaves. Serve with crusty bread.

Pork Schnitzel

This Croatian recipe features Central European ingredients.

INGREDIENTS

Serves 4

4 pork cutlets, about 7 ounces each
4 tablespoons olive oil
4 ounces chicken livers, chopped
1 garlic clove, crushed
all-purpose flour, seasoned, for coating
salt and freshly ground black pepper
1 tablespoon chopped fresh parsley
   to garnish

For the sauce

1 onion, thinly sliced
4 ounces bacon, thinly sliced
2 cups mixed wild mushrooms, sliced
½ cup olive oil
1 teaspoon mustard
⅔ cup white wine
½ cup sour cream
1 cup heavy cream
salt and freshly ground black pepper

1 Place the pork between 2 sheets of dampened plastic wrap or waxed paper and flatten with a meat mallet or rolling pin until about 6 × 4 inches. Season well.

2 Heat half the oil in a frying pan and cook the chicken livers and garlic for 1–2 minutes. Remove, drain on paper towels and let cool.

—— COOK'S TIP ——

If desired, replace the pork with veal or chicken and cook in the same way.

3 Divide the livers evenly between the four prepared pork cutlets and roll up into neat parcels. Secure with toothpicks or string before rolling lightly in the seasoned flour.

4 Heat the remaining oil and gently fry the schnitzels for 6–8 minutes on each side, or until golden brown. Drain on paper towels and keep warm.

5 Meanwhile, to make the sauce, sauté the onion, bacon and mushrooms in the oil for 2–3 minutes, then add the mustard, white wine and sour cream. Stir to the simmering point, then add the heavy cream and season.

6 Arrange the schnitzels on plates with a little of the sauce spooned around and the rest poured into a serving pitcher. Garnish with the parsley.

Spicy Rolled Beef

This recipe is a blend of Slovakian, Greek and Russian cuisines, with a spicy touch of coriander and peppercorns.

INGREDIENTS

Serves 4

4 thick 4–6-inch beef slices
¼ cup olive or vegetable oil,
   plus extra for frying
2 tablespoons black peppercorns,
   roughly crushed
2 tablespoons whole coriander seeds
1 onion, finely sliced
1¼ cups Bulgarian or dry red wine
1 egg, beaten
5-ounce can chopped tomatoes
polenta and sour cream, to serve

For the filling

½ cup minced ham
scant 1 cup bread crumbs
2 scallions, finely sliced
3 tablespoons chopped fresh parsley
1 egg yolk
3 ounces green bell pepper,
   seeded and finely chopped
¼ teaspoon ground allspice

1 Place the slices of beef between 2 sheets of dampened plastic wrap or waxed paper. Flatten with a meat mallet or rolling pin until the meat is evenly thin. Dip the slices in the oil.

2 Lay the meat out flat and sprinkle on the crushed peppercorns, coriander seeds and onion.

3 Roll up the meat neatly and place in a shallow glass or china dish. Pour on half of the wine, cover with plastic wrap and chill for 2 hours.

4 Meanwhile, combine all the filling ingredients together in a bowl and add a little water or beef stock if necessary, to moisten the stuffing.

5 Remove the beef from the bowl and shake off the spices and onion. Spoon 2–3 tablespoons of the filling into the middle of each piece of meat.

6 Brush the inner surface with egg and roll up well. Secure with a toothpick or tie with string.

7 Heat a little oil in a frying pan and sauté the rolls until brown on all sides. Reduce the heat and pour on the remaining wine and canned tomatoes. Simmer for 25–30 minutes or until the meat is tender. Season well and serve the beef with the sauce, the polenta and sour cream and plenty of cracked pepper. Garnish with a sprig of parsley.

Veal Cutlets

This simple dish is based on a German recipe, with the noodles adding a touch of the Mediterannean.

INGREDIENTS

Serves 4

4 veal cutlets, about 6 ounces each
²/₃ cup all-purpose flour, seasoned
2 eggs, beaten
scant 2 cups dry bread crumbs
2 tablespoons oil
4 tablespoons butter
coarsely ground white pepper
vegetable oil, for brushing
chives and paprika, to garnish
lemon wedges, buttered tagliatelle and
    green salad, to serve

1 Place the veal cutlets in between 2 sheets of dampened plastic wrap or waxed paper and flatten with a meat mallet or rolling pin until half as large again. Press a little ground white pepper into both sides of the cutlets.

2 Put the flour, eggs and bread crumbs on separate plates. Brush the meat with a little oil, then dip into the flour. Shake off any extra flour. Then dip the cutlets into the egg and then finally the bread crumbs. Set aside, loosely covered, for 30 minutes.

3 Heat the oil and half of the butter together in a large frying pan and gently fry the cutlets, one at a time, over low to medium heat for 3–4 minutes on each side. Be aware that too much heat will cause the veal to toughen. Keep the cutlets warm while you cook the remainder.

4 Top each cutlet with one-quarter of the remaining butter. Garnish with chives and a sprinkling of paprika. Serve with lemon wedges and buttered tagliatelle, with a green salad or vegetable, if desired.

COOK'S TIP

To prevent the bread crumb coating from cracking during cooking, use the back of a knife and lightly form a criss-cross pattern.

Romanian Kebab

Kebabs are popular worldwide, in part because they are so easily adapted to suit everyone's taste. In this modern version, lean lamb is marinated, then grilled with chunks of vegetables to produce a delicious, colorful and healthy meal. Traditionally, an unfermented grape juice (*mustarii*) and local bread is served with the meal.

INGREDIENTS

Serves 6

1½ pounds lean lamb, cut into
    1½-inch cubes
12 shallots or pearl onions
2 green bell peppers, seeded and cut
    into 12 pieces
12 small tomatoes
12 small mushrooms
sprigs of rosemary, to garnish
lemon slices, freshly cooked rice and
    crusty bread, to serve

For the marinade

juice of 1 lemon
½ cup red wine
1 onion, finely chopped
¼ cup olive oil
½ teaspoon each dried sage
    and rosemary
salt and freshly ground black pepper

1 For the marinade, combine the lemon juice, red wine, onion, olive oil, herbs and seasoning in a bowl.

2 Stir the cubes of lamb into the marinade. Cover and refrigerate for 2–12 hours, stirring occasionally.

3 Remove the lamb from the marinade and thread the pieces on to 6 skewers alternating with the onions, peppers, tomatoes and mushrooms.

COOK'S TIP

To vary this recipe sprinkle over 2 tablespoons chopped fresh parsley and finely chopped onion, to garnish.

4 Cook the kebabs over the hot coals of a grill or under a preheated broiler for 10–15 minutes, turning them once. Use the leftover marinade to brush over the kebabs during cooking to prevent the meat drying out.

5 Serve the kebabs on a bed of freshly cooked rice, sprinkled with fresh rosemary and accompanied by lemon slices and slices of crusty bread.

Chicken with Beans

This substantial Bulgarian casserole is bursting with flavor, texture and color.

INGREDIENTS

Serves 4–6

10 ounces dried kidney or other
  beans, soaked overnight
8–12 chicken pieces, such as thighs
  and drumsticks
12 strips bacon
2 large onions, thinly sliced
1 cup dry white wine
½ teaspoon chopped fresh sage
  or oregano
½ teaspoon chopped fresh rosemary
generous pinch of nutmeg
⅔ cup sour cream
1 tablespoon chili powder or paprika
salt and freshly ground black pepper
sprigs of rosemary, to garnish
lemon wedges, to serve

1 Preheat the oven to 350°F. Cook the beans in fast-boiling water for 20 minutes. Rinse and drain the beans well and trim the chicken pieces. Season the chicken with salt and pepper.

2 Arrange the bacon around the sides and base of an ovenproof dish. Sprinkle on half of the onion and then half the beans, followed by another layer of onion and then the remaining beans.

3 In a bowl combine the wine with half the fresh sage or oregano, rosemary and nutmeg. Pour on the onion and beans. In another bowl combine the sour cream and the chili powder or paprika.

4 Toss the chicken in the sour cream mixture and place on top of the beans. Cover with aluminum foil and bake for 1¼–1½ hours, removing the foil for the last 15 minutes of cooking. Serve garnished with rosemary and lemon.

Bulgarian Chicken

This is a traditional Bulgarian way of cooking chicken—in a flameproof pot, on top of the stove—so that it cooks slowly and evenly in its own juices.

INGREDIENTS

Serves 6–8

8 chicken pieces
6–8 firm ripe tomatoes, chopped
2 garlic cloves, crushed
3 onions, chopped
¼ cup oil or melted lard
1 cup good chicken stock
2 bay leaves
2 teaspoons paprika
10 white peppercorns, bruised
handful of parsley, stalks reserved and
  leaves finely chopped
salt

1 Put the chicken, tomatoes and garlic in the flameproof pot. Cover and cook gently for 10–15 minutes.

—— COOK'S TIP ——

For extra flavor add 1 finely seeded chopped chile pepper at Step 2.

2 Add the remaining ingredients, except the parsley leaves. Stir well.

3 Cover tightly and cook over very low heat, stirring occasionally, for 1¾–2 hours, or until the chicken is tender. Five minutes before the end of cooking, stir in the finely chopped parsley leaves.

Varna-style Chicken

In this tasty dish, the chicken is smothered in a rich, herb sauce.

INGREDIENTS

Serves 8
4-pound chicken, cut into 8 pieces
½ teaspoon chopped fresh thyme
3 tablespoons butter
3 tablespoons vegetable oil
3–4 garlic cloves, crushed
2 onions, finely chopped
salt and freshly ground white pepper
basil and thyme leaves, to garnish
freshly cooked rice, to serve

For the sauce
½ cup dry sherry
3 tablespoons tomato paste
a few fresh basil leaves
2 tablespoons white wine vinegar
generous pinch of sugar
1 teaspoon mild mustard
14-ounce can chopped tomatoes
3 cups mushrooms, sliced

1 Preheat the oven to 350°F. Season the chicken with salt, pepper and thyme. In a large frying pan cook the chicken in the butter and oil, until golden brown. Remove from the frying pan, place in an ovenproof dish and keep hot.

— COOK'S TIP —

Replace the cultivated mushrooms with wild mushrooms, if desired, but do make sure they are cleaned thoroughly before using.

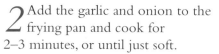

2 Add the garlic and onion to the frying pan and cook for 2–3 minutes, or until just soft.

3 For the sauce, combine the sherry, tomato paste, salt and pepper, basil, vinegar and sugar. Add the mustard and tomatoes. Pour into the frying pan and bring to a boil.

4 Reduce the heat and add the mushrooms. Adjust the seasoning with more sugar or vinegar to taste.

5 Pour the tomato sauce over the chicken. Bake, covered, for 45–60 minutes, or until cooked thoroughly. Serve on a bed of rice, garnished with basil and thyme.

Chicken Ghiveci

Romanians traditionally use a great variety of colorful seasonal vegetables in this hearty stew. A selection of home-grown herbs such as rosemary, marjoram and thyme, would also be added to flavor the stew.

INGREDIENTS

Serves 6

¼ cup vegetable oil or melted lard
1 mild onion, thinly sliced
2 garlic cloves, crushed
2 red bell peppers, seeded and sliced
about 3½-pound chicken
6 tablespoons tomato paste
3 potatoes, diced
1 teaspoon chopped fresh rosemary
1 teaspoon chopped fresh marjoram
1 teaspoon chopped fresh thyme
3 carrots, cut into chunks
½ small celeriac, cut into chunks
½ cup dry white wine
2 zucchini, sliced
salt and freshly ground black pepper
chopped fresh rosemary and
   marjoram, to garnish
dark rye bread, to serve

1 Heat the oil in a large flameproof casserole. Add the onion and garlic and cook for 1–2 minutes until soft; then add the red peppers.

2 Cut the chicken into 6 pieces, place in the casserole and brown gently on all sides.

3 After about 15 minutes add the tomato paste, potatoes, herbs, carrots, celeriac and white wine, and season to taste with salt and pepper. Cook over low heat, covered, for another 40–50 minutes.

4 Add the zucchini slices 5 minutes before the end of cooking. Adjust the seasoning to taste. Garnish with the herbs and serve with dark rye bread.

--- COOK'S TIP ---

If fresh herbs are unavailable, replace them with ½ teaspoon dried herbs.

Duckling Jubilee

This classic dish tastes delicious, and is very easily prepared.

INGREDIENTS

Serves 4
4½-pound duckling
¼ cup chopped fresh parsley
1 lemon, quartered
3 carrots, sliced
2 celery stalks, sliced
1 onion, roughly chopped
salt and freshly ground black pepper
apricots and sage flowers, to garnish

For the sauce
15-ounce can apricots in syrup
¼ cup sugar
2 teaspoons English mustard
¼ cup apricot jam
1 tablespoon lemon juice
2 teaspoons freshly grated lemon zest
¼ cup fresh orange juice
¼ teaspoon each ginger and coriander
4–5 tablespoons brandy

1 Preheat the oven to 425°F. Clean the duck well and pat dry with paper towels. Season the skin liberally.

2 Combine the chopped parsley, lemon, carrots, celery and onion in a bowl, then carefully spoon this into the cavity of the duck.

3 Cook the duck for 45 minutes on a trivet set over a roasting pan. Baste the duck occasionally with its juices.

4 Remove the duck from the oven and prick the skin well. Return it to the oven, reduce the temperature to 350°F, and cook for another 1–1½ hours or until the duck is golden brown, tender and crisp.

5 Meanwhile, put the apricots and their syrup, the sugar and mustard in a food processor or blender. Add the jam and process until smooth.

6 Pour the apricot mixture into a pan and stir in the lemon juice and zest, orange juice and spices. Bring to a boil, add the brandy and cook for another 1–2 minutes. Remove from heat and adjust the seasoning.

7 Discard the fruit, vegetables and herbs from inside the duck and arrange the bird on a serving platter. Garnish with fresh apricots and sage flowers. Serve the sauce separately.

COOK'S TIP

If using a frozen duck, make sure it is thoroughly thawed before cooking.

Turkey Zador with Mlinces

A Croatian recipe for special occasions, the unusual *mlinces* are used to soak up the juices.

INGREDIENTS

Serves 10–12
about 7-pound turkey, well thawed
   if frozen
2 garlic cloves, halved
4 ounces bacon, finely chopped
2 tablespoons chopped fresh rosemary
$\frac{1}{2}$ cup olive oil
1 cup dry white wine
bacon, to serve
sprigs of rosemary, to garnish

For the *mlinces*
3 cups all-purpose flour, sifted
$\frac{1}{2}$–$\frac{2}{3}$ cup warm water
2 tablespoons oil
sea salt

1 Preheat the oven to 400°F. Dry the turkey well inside and out using paper towels. Rub all over with the halved garlic.

2 Toss the bacon and rosemary together and use to stuff the turkey neck flap. Secure the skin underneath with a toothpick. Brush with the oil.

3 Place the turkey in a roasting pan and cover loosely with aluminum foil. Cook for 45–50 minutes. Remove the foil and reduce the oven temperature to 325°F.

4 Baste the turkey with the juices then pour on the white wine. Cook for 1 hour, basting occasionally with the juices. Reduce the temperature to 300°F, and continue to cook for another 45 minutes, basting the turkey well.

5 Meanwhile, make the *mlinces* by kneading the flour with a little salt and the water and oil to make a soft but pliable dough. Divide equally into 4.

6 Roll out the dough thinly on a lightly floured surface into 16-inch circles. Sprinkle with salt. Bake on baking sheets alongside the turkey for 25 minutes until crisp. Crush into pieces $2\frac{1}{2}$–4 inches.

7 6–8 minutes before the end of the cooking time for the turkey add the *mlinces* to the meat juices alongside the turkey. Serve with bacon, garnished with rosemary.

FISH

The numerous rivers, and the Adriatic and Black Seas that border the region, have traditionally provided an abundance of fish. Though these are not as well stocked today as they once were, classic Balkan cooking is proof of the wonderful variety of freshwater and ocean fish available from these natural sources. Carp is the predominant fish, but trout, swordfish and octopus are all popular. Many of these recipes rely on little more than herbs and spices, fresh vegetables or the local grain, mamaliga, *to create quick, healthy and tasty meals.*

Fish Baked in Dough

In this traditional rural recipe, the whole fish is encased in a yeast-based dough, which traps all the juices and flavor.

INGREDIENTS

Serves 4–6
about 2¼ pounds whole fish, such as
    red snapper, skinned and cleaned
sea salt
sprigs of fennel, to garnish
lemon wedges and zucchini and
    dill salad, to serve

For the dough
2 cups all-purpose flour, sifted
¼ teaspoon salt
¼-ounce envelope active dry yeast
1 egg, beaten
⅓–½ cup milk and warm water
    combined

1 Preheat the oven to 350°F. Pat the fish dry with paper towels and sprinkle inside and out with salt. Cover and chill the fish until the dough is ready for use.

2 Put the flour and salt into a large mixing bowl and stir in the yeast evenly. Make a well in the center. Whisk together the egg, milk and water, then pour half into the center of the flour. Knead to make a soft dough.

3 Knead the dough until smooth on a very lightly floured surface. Divide the dough in two parts, making one portion slightly larger than the other.

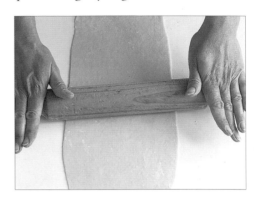

4 Carefully roll out the smaller piece of dough on a lightly floured surface to the shape of your fish, allowing a 2-inch border. Lay the dough on a large greased shallow baking sheet. Place the fish on top.

5 Roll out the remaining piece of dough until large enough to cover the fish, again allowing for a 2-inch border. Brush the edges of the pastry with water and seal well. Make criss-cross patterns across the top, using a sharp knife. Let rise for 30 minutes.

6 Glaze the dough with the remaining egg mixture. Make a small hole in the top of the pastry to let steam escape. Bake the fish for 25–30 minutes or until golden brown and well risen. Garnish with sprigs of fennel and serve with wedges of lemon and a salad of finely sliced zucchini, tossed in melted butter and sprinkled with dill seeds.

Swordfish Kebabs

Swordfish is a large ocean species found in Balkan waters, the Adriatic and the Black Seas. The firm, meaty flesh is ideal for charcoal grilling, poaching, steaming and baking.

INGREDIENTS

Serves 4

2 pounds swordfish, skinned
1 teaspoon paprika, plus extra
   to garnish
¼ cup lemon juice
3 tablespoons olive oil
6 fresh bay leaves
4 small tomatoes
2 green bell peppers, seeded and cut
   into 2-inch pieces
2 onions, cut into 4 wedges each
salt and freshly ground white pepper
extra bay leaves, to garnish
lettuce leaves, sour cream, cucumber
   salad and lime or lemon wedges,
   to serve

For the sauce
½ cup virgin olive oil
juice of 1 lemon
¼ cup finely chopped fresh parsley
salt and freshly ground black pepper

1 Cut the swordfish into 2-inch cubes and place in a shallow dish.

2 Combine the paprika, lemon juice, olive oil and seasoning and pour over the fish. Crush 2 bay leaves over the fish. Let sit, covered, in the refrigerator, for at least 2 hours.

3 Carefully turn the fish cubes in the marinade once or twice.

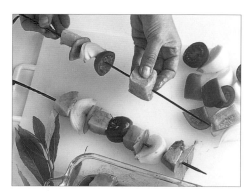

4 Thread the fish and vegetables on 4 large skewers; finish with a bay leaf.

5 Cook under a preheated broiler or over the hot coals of a barbecue, basting occasionally with any remaining marinade mixture. Turn the fish once during cooking.

6 Meanwhile, for the sauce, in a bowl whisk the oil, lemon juice, parsley and seasoning together until emulsified (thickened) and pour into a pitcher. Arrange the kebabs on lettuce leaves and serve with the parsley sauce, sour cream sprinkled with paprika, a cucumber salad and lime or lemon wedges and garnish with extra bay leaves, if desired.

COOK'S TIP

To help prevent the onion from falling apart during cooking, keep the root end intact when preparing the onion, so when you slice into it the root will hold the pieces together. Replace the swordfish with sturgeon, halibut or cod, if preferred.

Broiled Trout

These days, rainbow trout is largely a farmed fish, though it naturally dwells in the rivers, streams and lakes of the Balkans. Its pretty pink flesh and strong flavor encourages a very simple approach, like this one, when it comes to cooking it.

INGREDIENTS

Serves 4
¼ cup butter, melted
1 teaspoon chopped fresh dill
1 teaspoon chopped fresh
   flat-leaf parsley
4 trout fillets
3–4 tablespoons lemon juice
salt and freshly ground black pepper
baby red Swiss chard leaves and sprigs
   of flat-leaf parsley, to garnish

1 Stir together the butter, dill, flat-leaf parsley and seasoning.

COOK'S TIP

If using a grill, put the fish in a double-sided, hinged basket, which allows you to turn the fish over easily. To prevent the head and tail from burning, brush with a little water, then dip in granular salt.

2 Brush both sides of the fish with the herb butter before placing under a preheated broiler.

3 Broil for 5 minutes, then carefully turn over and cook the other side, basting with the remaining butter.

4 Just before serving, sprinkle on the lemon juice. Garnish with Swiss chard and sprigs of herbs.

Fish Parcels

Wrapping in parchment is a traditional method used by fishermen when cooking their lunch. They used to tie leaves or paper around the catch, dampen the parcel with water, bury it in hot ashes and cover it with a layer of hot coals.

INGREDIENTS

Serves 4
4 small sea bass or trout,
   about 14 ounces each
juice of 1 lemon
¼ cup butter, melted
a few sprigs of parsley or dill
½ fennel bulb, cut into strips
salt and freshly ground black pepper or
   cayenne pepper
cornbread and tomato and cucumber
   salad, to serve

1 Preheat the oven to 350°F, or prepare a grill. Remove the head, tail, fins and scales from the fish. Pat dry and season well. Sprinkle with lemon juice.

2 Cut out a double layer of waxed paper or baking parchment, large enough to put the fish in with enough extra to wrap around to seal. Brush the fish with the melted butter and place it in the center. Sprinkle with half the parsley or dill and the fennel.

3 Wrap up the fish loosely to make a neat parcel. Press down the edges securely. Bake for 15–20 minutes, depending on the thickness of the fish, or for 20–30 minutes if cooking on a grill.

4 Transfer the fish to serving plates and peel back the paper when ready to serve. Garnish with the remaining herbs and serve with slices of cornbread and a tomato and cucumber salad.

Carp Stuffed with Walnuts

Serve this elaborate dish on
December 6th for Saint Nikolas,
the patron saint of fishermen.

INGREDIENTS

Serves 10
about 3-pound whole carp, scaled,
   cleaned and roe reserved
coarse sea salt

For the stuffing
¾ cup walnut oil
1½ pounds onions, finely sliced
1 teaspoon paprika
pinch of cinnamon
1½ cups walnuts, chopped
1 tablespoon chopped fresh parsley
2 teaspoons fresh lemon juice
2 tomatoes, sliced
1 cup tomato juice
salt and freshly ground black pepper
walnuts and fennel sprigs, to garnish

1 Preheat the oven to 350°F. Sprinkle
the inside of the fish with a little
sea salt.

2 In a frying pan, heat the oil, then
cook the onions, paprika and
cinnamon together until soft.

3 Remove any membrane or skin
from the roe and roughly chop.

4 Add the roe and walnuts to the
frying pan and cook, stirring
constantly, for 5–6 minutes. Let cool
before stirring in the parsley and
lemon juice. Season to taste.

5 Fill the cavity of the fish with half
of the filling and secure with
toothpicks. Spoon the remaining
stuffing into the base of an ovenproof
dish and then place the fish on top.

6 Arrange the sliced tomatoes on
top of the fish and spoon on the
tomato juice. Bake for 30–45 minutes
or until the fish is browned and
flakes easily.

7 Carefully transfer to a serving plate.
Discard the toothpicks before
serving the fish sprinkled with extra
walnut pieces and sprigs of fennel.

Stuffed Red Snapper

There are a number of local flavors combined in this unusual recipe—the red snapper filled with carp, sharpened by the salty cheese and dill pickle.

INGREDIENTS

Serves 4

4 small red snapper, about 1 pound
    each, filleted and heads and
    fins removed
juice of 1 lemon
12 ounces fish fillets, such as carp, pike
    or sole, skinned
1 egg white
½ teaspoon chopped fresh tarragon
1 dill pickle, sliced
¾ cup fresh bread crumbs
¼ cup feta cheese or brinza,
    roughly crumbled
salt and freshly ground white pepper
2 tablespoons butter, melted
sprigs of tarragon or sweet cicely plus
    pansies or other edible flowers,
    to garnish
lemon wedges, to serve

1 Preheat the oven to 350°F. Wipe out the snapper and pat dry, removing any membrane with a little salt. Liberally rub the lemon juice inside the fish.

2 Put the fish fillets in a food processor and process with the egg white, tarragon, dill pickle, bread crumbs, cheese and a little ground white pepper, until a smooth paste is formed for the stuffing.

3 Using a spoon, fill the fish with the fish fillet mixture and lay them in an ovenproof dish.

4 Secure the fish with wooden skewers and bake for 40–50 minutes. Spoon on the melted butter halfway through cooking.

5 Transfer the fish carefully to a serving plate. Serve with lemon wedges and garnish with fresh sprigs of tarragon or sweet cicely and edible flowers, if desired.

VEGETABLES AND GRAINS

Eggplant, zucchini, hot peppers, cucumbers and tomatoes are just some of the vegetables that are available fresh in the Balkan markets. While some of the recipes in this section reflect Italian, Turkish or Greek influences, such as Zucchini with Rice and Stuffed Grape Leaves, others are uniquely Balkan. Mamaliga Baked with Cheese, using the local grain mamaliga, *is a perfect example of the versatility of this staple ingredient. The excellent* shopska *salads featuring the local yogurt are another typical delight.*

Creamy Eggplant and Mushrooms

This traditional way to serve eggplant may seem unusual to Western cooks, but is based on typical ingredients of the area.

INGREDIENTS

Serves 4–6
2 eggplant
½ cup unsalted butter
3 cups mushrooms, sliced
½ cup good strong beef stock
1 cup heavy cream
4 tablespoons chopped fresh parsley
salt and freshly ground white pepper
sour cream, to serve (optional)

1 Peel the eggplant with a sharp knife then slice into 3-inch long sticks, about ¼ inch thick.

2 Put the sticks on a dish towel and sprinkle liberally with salt.

3 Fold over the dish cloth to cover the eggplant and let sit for 30–35 minutes. Use the cloth to squeeze out the moisture from the eggplant.

4 Heat the butter in a large frying pan and cook the eggplant and mushrooms for 10 minutes. Pour in the beef stock and simmer for another 15 minutes, stirring occasionally.

5 Season to taste before stirring in the cream. Reheat but do not let boil. Add 3 tablespoons of the parsley and stir well. Spoon into a warm serving dish and garnish with the remaining parsley. Serve with sour cream, if desired.

COOK'S TIP

For a really smooth vegetable dish, carefully blend together the eggplant and mushrooms in a food processor or blender after the initial 10 minutes of cooking. Add the beef stock and follow the rest of the recipe.

Zucchini with Rice

This dish bears testimony to the influence of Italy, just on the other side of the Adriatic Sea, on Balkan cuisine.

INGREDIENTS

Serves 4 as a main course
8 as a side dish
2¼ pounds small or medium zucchini
4 tablespoons olive oil
3 onions, finely chopped
3 garlic cloves, crushed
1 teaspoon chili powder
14-ounce can chopped tomatoes
1 cup risotto or round-grain rice
2½–3 cups vegetable or chicken stock
2 tablespoons chopped fresh parsley
2 tablespoons chopped fresh dill
salt and freshly ground white pepper
sprigs of dill and olives, to garnish
thick plain yogurt, to serve

1 Preheat the oven to 375°F. Trim the zucchini and slice into large chunks.

2 Heat half the olive oil in a large pan and gently sauté the onions and garlic until just soft. Stir in the chili powder and tomatoes and simmer for 5–8 minutes before adding the zucchini and salt to taste.

3 Cook over low to medium heat for 10–15 minutes before stirring the rice into the pan.

4 Add the stock to the pan, cover and simmer for about 45 minutes or until the rice is tender. Stir the mixture occasionally.

5 Remove from heat and stir in pepper to taste, parsley and dill. Spoon into an ovenproof dish and bake for about 45 minutes.

6 Halfway through cooking, brush the remaining oil on the zucchini mixture. Garnish with the dill and olives. Serve with the yogurt.

COOK'S TIP

Add extra liquid as necessary, during step 5, to prevent the mixture from sticking.

Thracian Tomato Casserole

This is a typical recipe from the Thracian region of southern Bulgaria. It is eaten at harvest time during the hottest days of the year.

INGREDIENTS

Serves 4

2½ tablespoons olive oil
3 tablespoons chopped fresh
  flat-leaf parsley
2¼ pounds firm ripe tomatoes
1 teaspoon sugar
scant 1 cup day-old bread crumbs
½ teaspoon chili powder
  or paprika
salt
chopped parsley, to garnish
rye bread, to serve

1 Preheat the oven to 400°F. Brush a large baking dish with 1 tablespoon of the oil.

2 Sprinkle the chopped flat-leaf parsley on the bottom of the dish. Cut the tomatoes into even slices, discarding the two end slices of each. Arrange the slices of tomato in the dish so that they overlap slightly. Sprinkle them with a little salt and the sugar.

VARIATION

To vary this recipe, replace half the amount of tomatoes with 1 pound zucchini. Slice the zucchini evenly and arrange alternating slices of zucchini and tomato in the dish, overlapping the slices as before.

3 In a mixing bowl, stir together the bread crumbs, the remaining oil and chili powder or paprika, then sprinkle on top of the tomatoes.

4 Bake for 40–50 minutes, covering with aluminum foil if the topping is getting too brown. Serve hot or cold, garnished with chopped parsley and accompanied by rye bread.

Mixed Vegetable Casserole

INGREDIENTS

Serves 4

1 eggplant
½ cup okra, halved lengthwise
2 cups frozen or fresh peas
1½ cups green beans, cut into
  1-inch pieces
4 zucchini, cut into ½-inch pieces
2 onions, finely chopped
1 pound floury potatoes, diced into
  1-inch pieces
1 red bell pepper, seeded and sliced
14-ounce can chopped tomatoes
⅔ cup vegetable stock
¼ cup olive oil
5 tablespoons chopped fresh parsley
1 teaspoon paprika
salt

For the topping
3 tomatoes, sliced
1 zucchini, sliced

1 Preheat the oven to 375°F. Cut the eggplant into 1-inch pieces. Add the vegetables to a large oven-proof casserole.

2 Stir in the canned tomatoes, stock, olive oil, parsley, paprika and salt to taste. Stir well.

3 Level the surface of the vegetables and arrange alternate slices of tomatoes and zucchini attractively on top.

4 Put the lid on or cover the casserole dish tightly. Cook for 60–70 minutes. Serve either hot or cold with wedges of crusty bread.

Stuffed Grape Leaves

This vegetarian version of the famous Greek dish uses rice, pine nuts and raisins.

INGREDIENTS

Makes about 40
40 fresh grape leaves
¼ cup olive oil
lemon wedges and a crisp salad, to serve

For the stuffing
¾ cup long-grain rice, rinsed
2 bunches scallions, finely chopped
¼ cup pine nuts
scant ¼ cup seedless raisins
2 tablespoons chopped fresh mint leaves
¼ cup chopped fresh parsley
¾ teaspoon freshly ground black pepper
salt

1 Using a knife or a pair of scissors, snip off the thick, coarse stems from the grape leaves. Blanch the leaves in a large pan of boiling salted water until they just begin to change color. Drain and refresh in cold water.

2 Combine all the stuffing ingredients in a bowl.

3 Open out the grape leaves, ribbed-side facing up. Place a heaping teaspoonful of the stuffing on each.

--- COOK'S TIP ---

When fresh grape leaves are unavailable, use 2 packages of grape leaves preserved in brine and rinse and drain well before using.

4 Fold over the two outer edges to prevent the stuffing from falling out, then roll up the grape leaf from the stem end to form a neat roll.

5 Arrange the stuffed grape leaves neatly in a steamer and sprinkle on the olive oil. Cook over steam for 50–60 minutes or until the rice is completely cooked. Serve with lemon wedges and a salad, either cold as a *meze* or hot as an appetizer to a meal.

Stuffed Celeriac

Rather odd-looking, celeriac is a root vegetable that resembles an underdeveloped head of celery, and tastes a bit like sweet, nutty celery. It can be boiled in water or stock, and in this Romanian recipe, it is cooked in a mixture of olive oil and lemon-flavored water, giving it extra zest.

INGREDIENTS

Serves 4
4 small celeriac, 7–8 ounces each
juice of 2 lemons
²⁄₃ cup extra virgin olive oil
lemon wedges and sprigs of flat-leaf
   parsley, to garnish

For the stuffing
6 garlic cloves, finely chopped
1 teaspoon black peppercorns,
   finely crushed
4–5 tablespoons chopped
   fresh parsley
salt

1 Peel the celeriac carefully with a sharp knife and quickly immerse in a bowl of water and the lemon juice until ready to use.

COOK'S TIP

It is necessary to add the lemon juice to the water in order to help prevent the peeled celeriac from discoloring.

2 Reserve the lemon water. Very carefully scoop out the flesh of each celeriac, leaving a shell about ³⁄₄-inch thick, in which to put the filling.

3 Working quickly, chop up the scooped out celeriac flesh and mix with the garlic and peppercorns. Add the parsley and season with salt.

4 Fill the shells with the stuffing and sit them in a large pan, making sure they remain upright throughout cooking. Pour in the olive oil and enough lemon water to come halfway up the celeriac.

5 Simmer very gently until the celeriac are tender and almost all the cooking liquid has been absorbed. Serve the celeriac hot or cold with their juices, and garnish with lemon wedges and sprigs of parsley.

Mamaliga Baked with Cheese

Mamaliga, the local cornmeal, is first cooked to a porridge-like consistency, then baked with feta and the local cheese, *kashkaval*, to give it a pleasantly sharp taste.

INGREDIENTS

Serves 4–6
generous 1 cup coarse ground
    cornmeal
4 cups water
¼ cup unsalted butter
1½ cups feta cheese or *brinza*, drained
    and crumbled
½ cup hard *kashkaval* cheese, grated,
    for sprinkling
salt and freshly ground black pepper
bacon and scallions, sliced lengthwise,
    to garnish
tomato sauce, to serve

1 Preheat the oven to 375°F. Stirring occasionally, dry-fry the cornmeal in a large pan for 3–4 minutes or until it changes color. Remove from heat.

2 Slowly pour in the water and add a little salt. Return the pan to the heat and stir well until the cornmeal thickens a little. Cover, reduce the heat and let sit for 25 minutes, stirring often.

3 Remove from heat when thick enough to cause a wide trail to be left when a wooden spoon is lifted from the mixture. Stir in the butter, feta cheese or *brinza* and season well.

4 Spoon into an 8-inch greased springform pan. Bake for 25–30 minutes or until firm. Let sit overnight or for 2–3 hours. Serve sprinkled with *kashkaval* cheese, bacon and scallions, with tomato sauce.

Mamaliga Balls

A popular snack food, the *mamaliga* balls in this recipe contain bite-sized pieces of salami, but chunks of smoked ham or cheese are equally suitable.

INGREDIENTS

Serves 6–8
generous 2 cups fine cornmeal
2½ cups lightly salted water
generous pat of butter
1 cup salami, roughly chopped
oil, for deep frying
salt and freshly ground black pepper
pan-fried tomatoes and chopped fresh
    herbs, to serve

1 Stir the cornmeal and water together in a heavy saucepan. Bring to a boil and, stirring constantly, cook for 12 minutes or until suitable for rolling into balls. Stir in the butter and season well.

COOK'S TIP

Mamaliga is available in several grades, from coarse to fine. Coarse stoneground is often the best type for cooking.

2 With lightly floured hands, roll into balls double the size of a walnut and place the salami in the middle before sealing.

3 Fry the balls in the oil at 350–375°F, for 2–3 minutes or until golden brown. Drain well on paper towels. Serve with pan-fried tomatoes and chopped herbs.

Baked Cabbage

This economical dish uses the whole cabbage, including the core, where much flavor resides.

INGREDIENTS

Serves 4

1 green or white cabbage,
  about 1½ pounds
1 tablespoon light olive oil
2 tablespoons water
3–4 tablespoons vegetable stock
4 firm, ripe tomatoes, peeled
  and chopped
1 teaspoon mild chili powder
salt
1 tablespoon chopped fresh parsley or
  fennel, to garnish, optional

For the topping

3 firm ripe tomatoes, thinly sliced
1 tablespoon olive oil
salt and freshly ground black pepper

1 Preheat the oven to 350°F. Finely shred the leaves and the core of the cabbage. Heat the oil in a frying pan with the water and add the cabbage. Cook over very low heat, to let the cabbage sweat, for 5–10 minutes, with the lid on. Stir occasionally.

2 Add the stock and stir in the tomatoes. Cook for another 10 minutes. Season with the chili powder and a little salt.

3 Transfer the cabbage mixture to an ovenproof dish. Level the surface of the cabbage and arrange the sliced tomatoes on top. Season and brush with the oil to prevent them from drying out. Cook for 30–40 minutes or until the tomatoes are just starting to brown. Serve hot, garnished with a little parsley or fennel sprinkled on top, if desired.

COOK'S TIPS

To vary the taste, add seeded, diced red or green bell peppers to the cabbage with the tomatoes. If you have a shallow flameproof casserole, you could cook the cabbage in it on the stove and then simply transfer the casserole to the oven for baking.

Mashed Zucchini

Like eggplant, zucchini is a versatile vegetable. For extra texture and crunch, the zucchini in this recipe is covered in a light sprinkling of bread crumbs before broiling.

INGREDIENTS

Serves 4–6

6 zucchini, about 7 ounces each
5 tablespoons unsalted butter
1 onion, finely chopped
¼ cup day-old bread crumbs
salt
olives, lemon slices and sprig of
  parsley, to garnish

1 Trim the zucchini and cut into ½-inch slices. Add to a pan of boiling water and cook for 5–8 minutes or until just tender. Drain very well.

2 Using a potato masher, mash the zucchini or blend in a food processor or blender until smooth.

3 Melt 3 tablespoons of the butter in a frying pan and cook the onion until soft, then stir in the puréed zucchini. Cook without browning for another 2–3 minutes, before spooning into a warm ovenproof serving dish.

4 Dot the zucchini with the remaining butter and sprinkle on the bread crumbs. Cook under a preheated broiler until golden brown. Garnish with olives, lemon slices and a sprig of parsley just before serving.

--- COOK'S TIP ---

As an alternative, replace the zucchini with two large summer squashes that have been peeled, seeded and diced.

Cucumber and Tomato Salad

This Bulgarian *shopska* salad uses the excellent local yogurt. It is claimed that yogurt originated in Bulgaria. If unavailable, use plain yogurt instead.

INGREDIENTS

Serves 4
1 pound firm ripe tomatoes
½ cucumber
1 onion

For the dressing
¼ cup olive or vegetable oil
6 tablespoons thick plain yogurt
2 tablespoons chopped fresh parsley
    or chives
½ teaspoon vinegar
salt and freshly ground black pepper
1 small hot chile, seeded and chopped,
    or 1-inch lengths of chives,
    to garnish
country bread, to serve

1 Skin the tomatoes by first cutting a cross in the bottom of each tomato. Place in a bowl and cover with boiling water for 1–2 minutes or until the skin starts to split, then drain and plunge into cold water. Cut the tomatoes into quarters, seed and chop.

2 Chop the cucumber and onion into pieces the same size as the tomatoes and put them all in a bowl.

3 Combine all the dressing ingredients and season to taste. Pour over the salad, and toss all the ingredients together. Sprinkle on black pepper and the chopped chile or chives to garnish and serve with crusty bread.

Black Olive and Sardine Salad

The combined ingredients— sardines, olives, tomatoes and wine vinegar—bring a real burst of flavor to a delightful light summer salad.

INGREDIENTS

Serves 6
8 large firm ripe tomatoes
1 large red onion
¼ cup wine vinegar
6 tablespoons good olive oil
18–24 small sardines, cooked
¾ cup black pitted olives, drained well
salt and freshly ground black pepper
3 tablespoons chopped fresh parsley,
    to garnish

1 Slice the tomatoes into ¼-inch slices. Slice the onion thinly.

2 Arrange the tomatoes on a serving plate, overlapping the slices, then top with the red onion.

3 Combine the wine vinegar, olive oil and seasoning and spoon over the tomatoes.

4 Top with the sardines and black olives and sprinkle the chopped parsley on top.

— COOK'S TIP —

This recipe works equally well if the sardines are replaced with 6 shelled and halved hard-boiled eggs.

DESSERTS & BAKED GOODS

There is a wonderful range of desserts in the Balkan countries, ranging from simple Baked Peaches with cream to rich chocolate tortes, such as Torte Varazdin. Fresh fruit and nuts, such as walnuts and chestnuts, are popular ingredients and are often combined with sugar or honey to make sweet pastries. However, locally produced rose petals and rose water—simply served swirled through a rice pudding, for example—are perhaps the most distinctive addition to Balkan desserts.

Walnut and Coffee Cake

This two-layered cake has a rich walnut base and a creamy light coffee topping. Serve with a complementary drink, such as a sour cherry liqueur.

INGREDIENTS

Serves 8–12
4 sheets of phyllo pastry
¼ cup unsalted butter, melted
4 eggs, separated
scant 1 cup sugar
scant 1 cup walnuts, finely ground
walnut pieces and sifted confectioners'
    sugar, to decorate

For the topping
scant 1 cup unsalted butter,
    at room temperature
1 egg yolk
¾ cup sugar
3 tablespoons cold strong coffee

1 Preheat the oven to 350°F. Grease and line a deep 8-inch square cake pan. Brush the sheets of phyllo pastry with the butter, fold them over and place in the bottom of the prepared pan.

─── COOK'S TIPS ───

Please note that this recipe contains raw egg yolk. Use pistachios instead of the walnuts if preferred, grinding them in a processor.

2 Whisk the egg yolks and sugar in a mixing bowl until thick and pale, and the whisk leaves a trail.

3 Whisk the egg whites until stiff. Fold in the ground nuts.

4 Fold the egg white into the egg yolk mixture. Spoon into the prepared pan. Bake for 25–30 minutes until firm. Allow to cool.

5 Meanwhile, for the topping, cream the ingredients well. Spread on the cake with a round-bladed knife. Sprinkle on the walnut pieces. Chill for at least 3–4 hours or overnight. Sprinkle with confectioners' sugar and cut into fingers, triangles or squares.

Torte Varazdin

The classic chocolate cake is a favorite worldwide, and appears in many guises. In this version from the former Yugoslavia, it is enhanced with a creamy chestnut filling. Chill for about 60 minutes, if possible, before serving the cake.

INGREDIENTS

Serves 8–12
1 cup butter, at room temperature
generous 1 cup sugar
7 ounces semi-sweet chocolate, melted
6 eggs, separated
generous 1 cup all-purpose flour, sifted
chocolate curls, to decorate

For the filling
1 cup heavy cream, lightly whipped
1³⁄₄ cups canned chestnut purée
generous ¹⁄₂ cup sugar

For the topping
10 tablespoons unsalted butter
1¹⁄₄ cups confectioners' sugar, sifted
4 ounces semi-sweet chocolate, melted

1 Preheat the oven to 350°F. Grease and line the bottom and sides of an 8–9-inch round cake pan. Cream the butter and sugar together in a bowl until pale and fluffy. Stir in the melted chocolate and egg yolks. Fold the flour carefully into the chocolate mixture.

2 In a greasefree bowl, whisk the egg whites until stiff. Add a spoonful of the egg white to the chocolate mixture to loosen it, then carefully fold in the remainder. Spoon the cake mixture into the prepared pan.

3 Bake the cake for 45–50 minutes or until firm to the touch and a skewer inserted into the middle comes out clean. Cool on a wire rack. When cold, peel off the lining paper and slice the cake in half horizontally.

4 Meanwhile, gently combine the filling ingredients in a bowl. Sandwich the two cake halves together firmly with the chestnut filling.

5 In a mixing bowl, cream together the butter and sugar for the topping before stirring in the melted chocolate. Using a dampened knife spread the chocolate topping on the sides and top of the cake. Decorate with chocolate curls before serving.

Baklava

The origins of this recipe are in Greece and Turkey, but it has been adopted throughout southeastern Europe. It is a very sweet dessert, and black coffee is the perfect accompaniment.

INGREDIENTS

Makes 24 pieces
$^3/_4$ cup butter, melted
14-ounce package phyllo pastry, thawed if frozen
2 tablespoons lemon juice
$^1/_4$ cup honey
$^1/_4$ cup sugar
finely grated zest of 1 lemon
2 teaspoons cinnamon
$1^3/_4$ cups blanched almonds, chopped
$1^3/_4$ cups walnuts, chopped
$^3/_4$ cup pistachios or hazelnuts, chopped
chopped pistachios, to decorate

For the syrup
$1^3/_4$ cups sugar
$^1/_2$ cup honey
$2^1/_2$ cups water
2 strips of thinly pared lemon zest

1 Preheat the oven to 325°F. Brush the bottom of a shallow 12 × 8-inch jelly roll pan with a little of the melted butter.

2 Using the pan as a guide cut the sheets of phyllo pastry with a sharp knife to fit the pan exactly.

3 Place one sheet of pastry in the bottom of the pan, brush with a little melted butter, then repeat until you have used half of the pastry sheets. Set the remaining pastry aside and cover with a clean dish towel.

4 To make the filling, place the lemon juice, honey and sugar in a pan and heat gently until dissolved. Stir in the lemon zest, cinnamon and chopped nuts. Mix thoroughly.

5 Spread half the filling on the pastry, cover with 3 layers of the phyllo pastry and butter, then spread the remaining filling on the pastry.

6 Finish by using up the remaining sheets of pastry and butter on top, and brush the top of the pastry liberally with butter.

7 Using a sharp knife, carefully mark the pastry into squares, almost cutting through the filling. Bake in the preheated oven for 1 hour or until crisp and golden brown.

8 Meanwhile, make the syrup. Place the sugar, honey, water and lemon zest in a pan and stir over low heat until the sugar and honey have dissolved. Bring to a boil, then boil for another 10 minutes, until the mixture has thickened slightly.

9 Take the syrup off the heat and let cool slightly. Remove the baklava from the oven. Remove and discard the lemon zest from the syrup, then pour over the pastry. Let soak for 6 hours or overnight. Cut into squares and serve, decorated with chopped pistachios.

Currant Apple Mousse

This Romanian recipe uses locally grown apples and currants, macerated in red wine, to make this creamy mousse.

INGREDIENTS

Serves 4–6

¾ cup currants
¾ cup red wine, plus
    a little extra for topping up
4 crisp apples, cored, peeled
    and sliced
1 cup water
generous 1 cup sugar
2 tablespoons cornstarch
few drops of pink food
    coloring (optional)
3 egg yolks
1 teaspoon vanilla extract
¼ teaspoon cinnamon
2 egg whites
seedless red grapes, a little sugar and
    mint leaves, to decorate

1 Soak the currants in the red wine for 1–1½ hours. Drain the currants and set aside. Strain the wine through a fine sieve to remove most of the currant skins, then add more wine as necessary to bring back up to ¾ cup.

2 While the currants are soaking, put the apples in a pan and cook with the water and three-quarters of the sugar until soft. Let cool.

3 Purée the apples in a processor and then return to the pan.

4 Blend the cornstarch and the red wine and then pour into the apple purée. Cook for 8–10 minutes, stirring constantly. Add the food coloring, if using.

5 Beat the egg yolks in a bowl with the remaining sugar and the vanilla extract until pale and thick.

6 Whisk the apple mixture slowly into the egg yolks. Add the cinnamon and beat until smooth.

7 Refrigerate until thickened. Reserve 1 teaspoon of the egg white for decorating and whisk the remainder in a greasefree bowl, until stiff. Fold the currants and the whisked egg whites into the apple mixture and chill well.

8 While the mousse is chilling, make the frosted grapes. Brush the grapes with a little of the reserved egg white and sprinkle with sugar. Let dry. Use with the mint leaves to decorate the mousse.

Cherry Strudel

There are many varieties of strudel filling in this region, ranging from poppy seed, raisin and honey to sweet cheese. Cherry or apple strudels are among the most popular. A true strudel pastry is very thin, light and crispy, and takes a long time to roll out; nevertheless, it really is worth the effort.

INGREDIENTS

Serves 8–10
2¼ cups stone-ground flour
⅔ cup all-purpose flour
1 egg, beaten
10 tablespoons butter, melted
½ cup warm water
sifted confectioners' sugar, for dredging

For the filling
generous ½ cup walnuts, roughly
   chopped
generous ½ cup sugar
1½ pound cherries, pitted
scant 1 cup day-old bread crumbs

1 Preheat the oven to 400°F. Sift the flours together in a warm bowl. Make a well in the center, add the egg, ½ cup of the melted butter and the water. Mix into a smooth pliable dough, adding a little extra flour if needed. Let sit wrapped in plastic wrap for 30 minutes to rest.

2 Meanwhile, in a large bowl, combine the chopped walnuts, sugar, cherries and bread crumbs.

3 Lay out a clean dish towel and sprinkle it with flour. Carefully roll out the dough until it covers the towel. The dough should be as thin as possible, so that you can see the design on the cloth through it.

4 Dampen the edges with water. Spread the cherry filling on the pastry, leaving a gap all the way around the edge, about 1 inch wide. Roll up the pastry carefully, with the side edges folded in over the filling, to prevent it from coming out. Use the dish towel to help you roll the pastry.

5 Brush the strudel with the remaining melted butter. Place on a baking sheet and curl into a horseshoe shape. Cook for 30–40 minutes or until golden brown. Dredge with confectioners' sugar; serve warm or cold.

Boyer Cream

This light and fluffy mousse-like dessert is flavored with a hint of rose water.

INGREDIENTS

Serves 4–6
1 cup full-fat cream cheese
5 tablespoons sour cream
2 eggs, separated
$^1/_4$ cup vanilla sugar
$^2/_3$ cup raspberries
1 cup strawberries
sifted confectioners' sugar, to taste
1 tablespoon rose water
halved strawberries, mint leaves and
   small pink roses, to decorate

1 Beat the cream cheese in a bowl with the sour cream and egg yolks until the cheese has softened. Stir in half the sugar.

2 Whisk the egg whites in another bowl until stiff, then whisk in the remaining sugar. Fold the egg whites into the cream cheese mixture. Chill until ready for use.

3 To make the fruit sauce, purée the raspberries and strawberries. Sieve to remove seeds; add confectioners' sugar, to taste. Swirl 4–6 glass dishes with a little rose water and divide three-quarters of the sauce between the dishes. Top with the cream cheese mixture. Add the remaining sauce in spoonfuls, swirling it into the cream cheese.

4 Place the dishes on saucers and decorate with halved strawberries, mint leaves and small roses.

Bulgarian Rice Pudding

There are many versions of rice pudding to choose from, but the presence here of pistachios, lemon, cinnamon and rose petals, makes this version a distinctly Bulgarian one.

INGREDIENTS

Serves 4–6
scant $^1/_2$ cup short-grain
   or pudding rice
3 tablespoons sugar
$3^3/_4$ cups whole milk
2 tablespoons unsalted butter
1 cinnamon stick
strip of lemon zest
halved pistachios and rose petals,
   to decorate

1 Put the rice, sugar, milk, butter, cinnamon stick and lemon zest into a large heavy pan.

COOK'S TIP

For an extra creamy rice pudding, fold in $^2/_3$ cup lightly whipped heavy cream just before serving.

2 Cook over very low heat, stirring occasionally, for about $1^1/_2$ hours or until thick and creamy. Remove and discard the cinnamon stick and lemon zest.

3 Spoon into serving dishes and sprinkle with halved pistachios and rose petals, to decorate.

Lemon Cake

This simple, pleasing Romanian cake is made from a blend of thick yogurt, lemon and honey, with a hint of cinnamon.

INGREDIENTS

Makes 16
$^1/_4$ cup butter, softened
generous $^1/_2$ cup sugar
2 large eggs, separated
$^1/_2$ cup plain yogurt
grated zest of 2 lemons
juice of $^1/_2$ lemon
$1^1/_4$ cups self-rising flour
$^1/_2$ teaspoon baking powder
curls of lemon zest, to decorate

For the syrup
juice of $^1/_2$ lemon
$^1/_4$ cup honey
3 tablespoons water
1 small cinnamon stick

1 Preheat the oven to 375°F. Grease and line a shallow 7-inch square cake pan. Cream together the softened butter and sugar in a bowl until pale and fluffy.

2 Slowly add the egg yolks, yogurt and lemon zest and juice. Beat until smooth. In a separate, greasefree bowl, whisk the egg whites until just stiff.

3 Sift together the flour and baking powder. Fold into the yogurt mixture, then fold in the egg whites.

4 Spoon the mixture into the prepared cake pan. Bake for about 25 minutes or until golden brown and firm to the touch. Turn out onto a plate and peel off the paper.

5 Meanwhile, to make the syrup, put the lemon juice, honey, water and cinnamon stick in a small pan. Stir until boiling, then cook until the mixture is syrupy.

6 Remove the pan from heat. Remove and discard the cinnamon stick. Spoon the warm syrup on the cake, then sprinkle with the lemon zest. Let cool completely before cutting into 16 pieces.

COOK'S TIP

The local honey has a perfumed flavor due to the pollen collected from the wild plants in the foothills of the fruit orchards. Try to use scented honey in this dish.

Citrus Ricotta Squares

This light cheesecake has a sponge cake layer on top and on the bottom and a creamy ricotta cheese filling with a hint of citrus.

INGREDIENTS

Makes 16
3 large eggs, separated
scant 1 cup sugar
3 tablespoons hot water
1²/₃ cups all-purpose flour, sifted
½ teaspoon baking powder
confectioners' sugar, sifted,
   for dredging
long strands of lemon zest,
   to decorate
fresh fruit, to serve

For the filling
2½ cups ricotta cheese
½ cup heavy cream, lightly whipped
2 tablespoons sugar
2 teaspoons lemon juice

1 Preheat the oven to 375°F. Grease a 12 × 8-inch jelly roll pan. Whisk together the egg yolks and sugar in a large bowl until the mixture is pale and the whisk leaves a trail when lifted. (The mixture should triple in volume.)

COOK'S TIP

An ideal way of serving the citrus ricotta squares is with seasonal fruits such as blackberries, peaches or apricots, soaked in a little cherry brandy (*maraska*).

2 Fold the hot water into the egg yolks, together with the flour and baking powder. Lightly whisk the egg whites in a greasefree bowl and then fold these into the egg yolks.

3 Pour the sponge mixture into the prepared pan, tilting it to help ease the mixture into the corners. Bake for 15–20 minutes or until golden brown and firm to the touch. Turn out and cool on a wire rack, then carefully slice in half horizontally.

4 Make the filling by beating the ricotta cheese in a bowl and then stirring in the cream, sugar and lemon juice. Spread the filling on top of the base, then top with the remaining half of the cake. Press down lightly on the top layer.

5 Chill the cake for 3–4 hours. Just before serving, dredge with a little confectioners' sugar and decorate with the lemon zest. Cut into 16 squares and serve with fresh fruit.

Baked Peaches

This Bulgarian recipe uses fresh peaches with a hint of cloves to give an aromatic, spicy flavor. Peaches are plentiful in summer, so they are either dried, used in wines or brandy, or bottled to preserve them for use later on.

INGREDIENTS

Serves 6
3 tablespoons unsalted butter
6 firm ripe peaches, washed
12 whole cloves
$^{1}/_{2}$ cup vanilla sugar
3 tablespoons brandy or dry white
  wine (optional)
pistachios, mint leaves and a little sifted
  confectioners' sugar, to decorate
whipped cream, to serve

1 Preheat the oven to 350°F. Spread half the butter in an ovenproof dish, making sure both the sides and bottom are well coated.

2 Halve the peaches and remove the pit. Place the peaches skin-side down in the dish. Push a whole clove into the center of each peach half.

3 Sprinkle with the sugar and dot the remaining butter into each peach half. Drizzle on the brandy or wine, if using. Bake for 30 minutes or until the peaches are tender.

4 Serve the peaches, hot or cold, with freshly whipped cream, pistachios and sprigs of mint, and sprinkle with a little confectioners' sugar.

Halva

Halva is the name for a candy made throughout the Balkans. It can be based on wheat flour, cornmeal, semolina or rice flour, with different proportions of butter, milk, water and sugar. If you are new to *halva*, this is a good basic version to start off with.

INGREDIENTS

Serves 6–8
$1^{1}/_{2}$ cups fine-grained semolina
$^{1}/_{4}$ cup butter
$^{1}/_{4}$ cup sugar
3 cups very hot milk
grated zest of 1 lemon
$^{1}/_{2}$ cup walnuts, chopped
chopped walnuts and halved
  pistachios, to decorate
cinnamon, for sprinkling

1 Dry-fry the semolina carefully in a very heavy saucepan over low heat for about 5 minutes, stirring continuously, or until the mixture turns a golden color. Do not let it brown. Remove from heat and add the butter and sugar, stirring until melted.

COOK'S TIP

Take care when dry-frying the semolina so it does not burn on the bottom of the pan.

2 Return to low heat and gradually add the milk to the pan, mixing well between each addition. Simmer for 5 minutes, then stir in the lemon zest and walnuts.

3 Simmer for 5 more minutes, stirring constantly, until very thick. Cover and set aside for 2–3 minutes.

4 Fluff up the mixture with a fork. Serve warm, decorated with walnuts, pistachios and cinnamon.

Balkan Doughnuts

These flour-based doughnuts are a natural extension of the Eastern European love for dumplings. They are also the ideal showcase for homemade jam and are usually filled with a thick fruity jam, such as cherry, plum or apricot. Ideally, eat the doughnuts on the day of making.

INGREDIENTS

Makes 10–12
2 cups all-purpose flour, warmed
$^1/_2$ teaspoon salt
$^1/_4$-ounce envelope active dry yeast
1 egg, beaten
4–6 tablespoons milk
1 tablespoon sugar
$^1/_4$ cup cherry jam
oil, for deep frying
$^1/_4$ cup sugar
$^1/_2$ teaspoon cinnamon

1 Sift the flour into a bowl with the salt. Stir in the yeast. Make a well and add the egg, milk and sugar.

2 Combine well to form a soft dough, adding a little more milk if necessary, to make a smooth, but not sticky, dough.

3 Beat well, cover with plastic wrap and set aside for 1–1$^1/_2$ hours in a warm place to rise until the dough has doubled in size.

4 Knead the dough on a lightly floured surface and divide it into 10–12 pieces.

5 Shape each into a round and put 1 teaspoon of jam in the center.

6 Dampen the edges of the dough with water, then draw them up to form a ball, pressing firmly to ensure that the jam will not escape during cooking. Place on a greased baking sheet and let rise for 15 minutes.

7 Heat the oil in a large saucepan to 350°F or until a 1-inch piece of bread turns golden in 60–70 seconds. Fry the doughnuts for 5–10 minutes, until golden brown. Drain well on paper towels.

8 Mix the sugar and cinnamon together on a plate or in a plastic bag and use to liberally coat the doughnuts.

Bird of Paradise Bread

This Bulgarian bread, enriched with eggs and cheese, is named after its traditional decoration.

INGREDIENTS

Serves 10–12

1 tablespoon active dry yeast
¼ cup lukewarm water
3 cups all-purpose flour, sifted
1½ teaspoons salt
6 tablespoons plain yogurt
5 eggs, beaten
⅓ cup feta cheese or *brinza*, finely chopped
1 tablespoon milk

For the topping

4 ounces *kashkaval* or Cheddar cheese, sliced into 4 triangles
thick piece of ham, cut into 4 × 1-inch squares
4 pitted black olives (optional)
about 1-inch star shape cut out of red bell pepper

1 Sprinkle the yeast on the warm water in a small bowl. Let stand for 2–3 minutes, stir well, then set aside for 5–10 minutes until frothy.

2 Sift the flour and salt into a bowl. Make a well in the center and pour in the yeast mixture, yogurt, 4 of the eggs and the feta cheese or *brinza*. Stir well together to form a dough, adding a little extra flour if necessary. Knead well on a lightly floured surface for about 10 minutes.

3 Shape the dough into an even ball, cover with plastic wrap and set in a warm place to rise until doubled in size, about 2 hours.

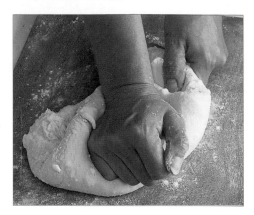

4 On a lightly floured surface gently knead the dough again and shape into a round to fit in a greased 8-inch springform pan, or place directly on a lightly buttered baking sheet. In a bowl, beat the 1 remaining egg with the milk and brush liberally on the loaf.

5 To decorate the loaf, arrange the cheese triangles evenly on top to form a square in the middle. Place the ham and olives, if using, in between the cheese and put the star of red pepper in the center. Let rise for another 30–45 minutes. Preheat the oven to 400°F, then bake for 15 minutes.

6 Reduce the temperature to 350°F and bake for another 30–40 minutes or until golden brown. Cool on a wire rack.

Mamaliga Bread

Mamaliga, or cornmeal, is one of the staple ingredients of the Balkan area. Cheese can be added to this light golden bread to give it a savory taste.

INGREDIENTS

Makes 1 loaf or 9 small buns
²/₃ cup self-rising flour
1½ teaspoons baking powder
¾ cup cornmeal
½ teaspoon salt
1 egg
²/₃ cup milk
¼ cup Cheddar cheese,
    finely grated (optional)

1 Preheat the oven to 400°F. Place the self-rising flour, baking powder, cornmeal and salt in a large mixing bowl. Mix well, then make a well in the center.

2 Add the egg, milk and Cheddar cheese, if using. Mix well with a wooden spoon.

3 Pour the mixture into a greased 6-inch round cake pan or a 9-hole muffin pan.

4 Bake for 20–25 minutes or until well risen, golden and firm to the touch. Cool briefly on a wire rack. Serve warm in thick slices.

COOK'S TIP

Cook this loaf immediately after making, otherwise the rising agent will be less effective and the loaf will not be as light.

INDEX

A

acorn squash: lamb-stuffed
squash, 194
Adriatic, 172–251
desserts and baked
goods, 234–51
fish, 208–19
ingredients, 176–7
meat and poultry, 192–207
soups and appetizers, 178–91
vegetables and grains, 220–33
alcohol, 10–11, 17, 97, 177
ale: carp in black sauce, 129
pork and garlic sausage
casserole, 116
almonds: apricot treat, 84
baklava, 238
layered pancake gâteau, 164
Lebkuchen, 169
Linzertorte, 155
plum and almond tart, 86
poppy seed roll, 91
stollen, 170
tort Migdalowy, 80
appetizers: Germany, Austria,
Hungary and the Czech
Republic, 106–9
Romania, Bulgaria and the
East Adriatic, 184–91
Russia, Poland and the
Ukraine, 26–33
apples: apple crêpes, 160
apple soup, 182
apple strudel, 154
currant apple mousse, 240
Himmel und Erde, 141
pork and garlic sausage
casserole, 116
roast goose with apples, 125
roast loin of pork with apple
stuffing, 37
spicy apple cake, 161
stewed fruit, 166
apricots: apricot treat, 84
duckling jubilee, 206
Austria, 92–171
desserts and baked
goods, 150–71
fish, 126–37

ingredients, 96–7
meat and poultry, 110–25
soups and appetizers, 98–109
vegetables and grains, 138–49

B

babka, 88
babka, fish, 54
bacon: baked carp, 133
buckwheat kasha, 68
carters' millet, 68
chicken with beans, 202
galushki, 64
halibut cooked under
cream, 132
lentil soup, 101
liver and bacon varenyky, 36
meatloaf, 196
pork and garlic sausage
casserole, 116
pork schnitzel, 198
Somogy beans, 144
spiced red cabbage, 148
turkey zador with
mlinces, 207
veal roast, 118
baklava, 238
Balkan doughnuts, 248
barley: braised barley and
vegetables, 67
pea and barley soup, 20
Bavarian cream, 162
Bavarian potato dumplings, 146
beans, 177
chicken with beans, 202
Somogy beans, 144
beef: beef Stroganov, 38
bigos, 40
Bulgarian rolled beef, 199
Hungarian goulash, 119
kotlety, 38
kovbasa, 41
meatloaf, 196
roast beef marinated in
vegetables, 120
Russian hamburgers, 38
sauerbraten, 122
spicy rolled beef, 199
beets: beet casserole, 70
borscht, 21
grated beet and celery
salad, 72
bell peppers: eggplant and bell
pepper spread, 188
baked carp, 133
broiled pepper salad, 190

chicken ghiveci, 205
fish goulash, 130
fried bell peppers with
cheese, 185
Hungarian goulash, 119
Lecsó, 145
lamb goulash with tomatoes
and peppers, 113
Romanian kebab, 201
swordfish kebabs, 211
Bessarabian crêpes, 186
bigos, 40
pork and garlic sausage
casserole, 116
bird of paradise bread, 250
bitki, chicken, 44
black bread, 171
Black Forest cherry cake, 152
black olive and sardine salad, 232
black pudding: Himmel und
Erde, 141
black sauce, carp in, 129
blini, buckwheat, 31
blue trout, 134
borscht, 21
Boyer cream, 242
bread, 9, 17
bird of paradise bread, 250
black bread, 171
kulich, 76
mamaliga bread, 251
sour rye bread, 90
tarama, 188
buckwheat blini, 31
buckwheat kasha, 68
Bulgaria, 172–251
desserts and baked
goods, 234–51
fish, 208–19
ingredients, 176–7
meat and poultry, 192–207
soups and appetizers, 178–91
vegetables and grains, 220–33
Bulgarian chicken, 202
Bulgarian lamb in pastry, 195
Bulgarian rice pudding, 242
Bulgarian rolled beef, 199
Bulgarian sour lamb soup, 181
burgers: kotlety, 38
buttermilk: black bread, 171

C

cabbage: baked cabbage, 230
fresh cabbage shchi, 22
Muscovite solyanka, 55

spiced red cabbage, 148
see also sauerkraut
cakes, 95
babka, 88
Black Forest cherry cake, 152
citrus ricotta squares, 245
Dobos torta, 156
Lebkuchen, 169
lemon cake, 244
nut squares, 168
Polish honey cake, 78
spicy apple cake, 161
stollen, 170
tort Migdalowy, 80
torte Varazdin, 237
candied peel: apricot treat, 84
Lebkuchen, 169
paskha, 77
poppy seed roll, 91
candy: halva, 246
caraway seeds, 97
poached carp with caraway
seeds, 215
carp: baked carp, 133
carp in black sauce, 129
carp with green horseradish
sauce, 56
carp stuffed with walnuts, 218
poached carp with caraway
seeds, 215
stuffed red snapper, 219
carters' millet, 68
casseroles and stews: beet
casserole, 70
bigos, 40
braised tench and
vegetables, 52
Bulgarian chicken, 202
chicken ghiveci, 205
fish goulash, 130
fish stew and herbed mashed
potatoes, 216
lamb goulash with tomatoes
and bell peppers, 113

soups and appetizers, 98–109
vegetables and grains, 138–49
gherkins: leg of lamb with pickle
sauce, 112
ghiveci, chicken, 205
glacé cherries: stollen, 170
golden raisins: babka, 88
goose: roast goose with
apples, 125
goulash: fish goulash, 130
Hungarian goulash, 119
lamb goulash with tomatoes
and bell peppers, 113
grains, 10, 17, 96, 177
grandfather's soup, 25
grape leaves, stuffed, 226
green beans: vegetable salad, 109
grey mullet: fish baked in
dough, 210
grouse: Olivier salad, 32

H
halibut cooked under cream, 132
halva, 246
ham: bird of paradise bread, 250
Bulgarian rolled beef, 199
kohlrabi baked with ham, 142
veal roast, 118
hamburgers, Russian, 38
hazelnuts: plum streusel
slices, 163
Polish honey cake, 78
roast goose with apples, 125
herbs, 17, 96–7, 177
herbed liver pâté pie, 108
herring pâté , 28
Himmel und Erde, 141
honey: baklava, 238
Polish honey cake, 78
roast duckling with honey, 47
spiced red cabbage, 148
horseradish: baked cod with
horseradish sauce, 58
carp with green horseradish
sauce, 56
Hungarian goulash, 119

Hungarian sour cherry soup, 104
Hungary, 92–171
desserts and baked
goods, 150–71
fish, 126–37
ingredients, 96–7
meat and poultry, 110–25
soups and appetizers, 98–109
vegetables and grains, 138–49

I
ingredients, 9–11
Germany, Austria, Hungary
and the Czech
Republic, 94–7
Romania, Bulgaria and the
East Adriatic, 174–7
Russia, Poland and
Ukraine, 14–17

K
kasha, buckwheat, 68
kashkaval, 176
kebabs: Romanian kebab, 201
swordfish kebabs, 211
kisel, cheesecake with, 158
kohlrabi baked with ham, 142
kotlety, 38
kovbasa, 41
kulich, 76
kulybyaka, salmon, 51

L
lamb: Bulgarian lamb in
pastry, 195
Bulgarian sour lamb soup, 181
field-roasted lamb, 42
lamb goulash with tomatoes
and bell peppers, 113
lamb meatball soup with
vegetables, 184

lamb plov, 43
lamb-stuffed squash, 194
leg of lamb with pickle
sauce, 112
Romanian kebab, 201
layered pancake gâteau, 164
Lebkuchen, 169
Lecsó, 145
lemon: lemon cake, 244
stuffed celeriac, 227
lentil soup, 101
lepeshki, 87
Linzertorte, 155
liqueurs, 97
little finger cookies, 28
liver: herbed liver pâté pie, 108
liver and bacon varenyky, 36
lumpfish roe: buckwheat
blini, 31

M
mackerel: mackerel in wine
sauce, 216
see also smoked mackerel
mamaliga: mamaliga baked with
cheese, 228
mamaliga balls, 228
mamaliga bread, 251
marinated fish, 136
marzipan: stollen, 170
mashed zucchini, 231
meat and poultry: Germany,
Austria, Hungary and
the Czech Republic,
95, 96, 110–25
Romania, Bulgaria and the
East Adriatic, 192–207
Russia, Poland and the
Ukraine, 16, 34–47
see also beef, veal etc.
meatloaf, 196
meatballs: chicken bitki, 44
lamb meatball soup with
vegetables, 184
meze, 174
millet, carters', 68
mint: stuffed grape leaves, 226

mlinces, turkey zador with, 207
mousses: currant apple
mousse, 240
pike and salmon mousse, 50
Muscovite solyanka, 55
mushrooms, 16
baked pike with wild
mushrooms, 128
beet casserole, 70
braised tench and
vegetables, 52
carters' millet, 68
chicken in Badacsonyi
wine, 124
chicken bitki, 44
chicken with wild mushrooms
and garlic, 123
creamy eggplant and
mushrooms, 222
mixed mushroom solyanka, 24
pork schnitzel, 198
rolled fish fillets, 56
Romanian kebab, 201
stuffed mushrooms with
spinach, 106
uszka, 71
Varna-style chicken, 204
mustard sauce, cod in, 137

N
noodles, drop, 25
nuts, 177
nut squares, 168
see also almonds, walnuts etc.

O
octopus salad, 191
olives: black olive and sardine
salad, 232
octopus salad, 191
Olivier salad, 32
onions: carp stuffed with
walnuts, 218
onion and fish casserole, 214
swordfish kebabs, 211
see also scallions, shallots

P
pampushki, 63
pancakes: layered pancake
gâteau, 164
potato pancakes, 107
paper parcels, fish, 212